High Tea

AT THE VICTORIA ROOM

High Tea

AT THE VICTORIA ROOM

JILL JONES-EVANS AND JOE GAMBACORTA

NH
NEW
HOLLAND

DEDICATION

To all the staff at The Victoria Room past, present and future—an enormous thank you for making our dream a reality and for all your support, loyalty and dedication.

ACKNOWLEDGEMENTS

Our heartfelt thanks and appreciation go to Valerie Christopher, Holly Jones-Evans, Ashley Jones-Evans, Lindsay Jones-Evans, Chrystalla Gambacorta, Devita Tjondro and all the kitchen brigade, Lee Cavanagh Potter, Margarita Peker, Kristy Clark, Charlotta Ward and Virginia Dowzer.

Contents

Introduction

High Tea is quite simply a ritual of pleasure and elementary decadence. Delicious and fun, High Tea is an afternoon treat that satisfies the most basic desires of the palate whilst providing the perfect excuse for a gathering of friends or family.

High Tea first gained popularity almost two centuries ago, but has in recent years witnessed something of a worldwide social revival.

Now, after six years of award-winning service, The Victoria Room is revealing the High Tea tricks of the trade. Since 2003, the opulent British Raj decor of the bar restaurant has welcomed thousands of patrons each year to delight in an experience that is both luxurious and entertaining.

Over the years we have hosted wedding receptions, baby showers, bridal showers, 21st birthdays, 60th birthdays, reunions, Christmas parties, children's birthday parties and even a few marriage proposals! I am genuinely honoured that so many people have chosen to celebrate these exciting and meaningful life events with us during High Tea.

There is still something very special and magical about High Tea. It is because of this, in my belief, that patrons have chosen to perpetuate the festive feel by using it as a social conduit for other exciting events. High Tea has been enjoyed for all occasions; from simple and friendly get togethers to fashion and product launches.

Hosting High Tea has given my partners, the staff and myself at The Victoria Room incredible amounts of joy and satisfaction, and we all hope to be serving happy customers for years to come. This book will provide you with all the knowledge and advice needed to recreate an at-home version of an event that is fast becoming one of the world's most loved weekend activities.

Jill Jones-Evans

The History of High Tea

It was around 1830 when the ritual of 'Afternoon Tea' is said to have been established by Anna Maria Stanhope, the 7th Duchess of Bedford. With lunch served at noon and dinner not eaten until 8 o'clock at night, the Duchess would order the kitchen to prepare a tray of tea, pastries, bread and jams around mid-afternoon. It became an adored habit, and as most aristocratic men were enjoying light meals and refreshments at their gentlemen's clubs, the Duchess took to inviting her lady friends to join her for Afternoon Tea at Belvoir Castle. Being a lady-in-waiting for Queen Victoria, the Duchess had soon set a trend amongst the upper class and by the early 1840s the term Afternoon Tea was widely used.

High Tea, meanwhile, was a daily affair for the working classes who did not have the time or the wealth to enjoy the delicate pleasures of Afternoon Tea. They had a full meal at midday while at work, and would then prepare an evening meal or 'tea' around 6 o'clock. This meal would be served at a 'high table' and would consist of bread, cheese, cold meats and eggs, and—of course—a nice pot of hot tea. This soon became referred to as High Tea.

Today the term High Tea commonly refers to the earlier practice of Afternoon Tea, where tea is served from mid-afternoon to early evening along with a selection of sweet and savoury finger foods. Fortunately for most, the luxuries that were once exclusively reserved for the upper echelons of society are now available to be enjoyed by one and all.

HIGH TEA ETIQUETTE

It's fun to review some of the optional etiquette of a High Tea party.

Invitation: Originally, an invitation to a 'tea party' was written and sent by post and this tradition should be adhered to where possible. In today's age of technology there is nothing finer than to receive a hand-written invitation in your letterbox, rather than in the inbox of your computer. As stationery has become somewhat of a luxury item, there are now so many beautiful designs and textures from which to choose, so there is no excuse. However, if one finds oneself pressed for time, a nicely drafted email or text message is acceptable (just).

Dress: Tea drinking prompted silversmiths and linen manufacturers to produce appropriate tableware and even tea gowns were designed. Today, the dress code for High Tea is still smart, although ladies are not expected to wear dresses, hats and gloves. Gentlemen are, however, required to wear a jacket and tie in most formal teahouses around the world.

Napery: The hostess signals the commencement of service by taking her napkin off the plate and placing it in her lap. Guests then follow. Paper napkins are acceptable, but top quality linen is preferred. Crisp, white linen napkins are best for a formal High Tea , though ladies are reminded to blot their lipstick before dabbing to avoid leaving stains on the linen. Table cloths are optional, depending on the style of table. The hostess will signal the conclusion of service by placing her napkin loosely to the table or plate.

Cutlery: A knife and fork may be used together to consume an open sandwich, but not a closed sandwich and never on a scone. If pastries are served, a knife and fork are also fine to use. The licking of one's knife is not permitted, nor the licking of the back of one's spoon!

Tea etiquette: To drink your tea, lift the cup and saucer together—holding the saucer in one hand and cup in the other. Slip your index finger through the handle of the teacup, almost to the first knuckle, then balance and secure the cup by placing your thumb on the top of the handle, allowing the bottom of the handle to rest on your middle finger. The ring and pinkie fingers should not be extended, but should rest by curving gently back toward your wrist. Hold the saucer under your cup while you sip your tea. If you are at a buffet tea, hold the tea saucer in your lap with your left hand and hold the teacup in your right hand. Do not to sip your tea from the spoon or the saucer and avoid clinking the sides of the cup whilst stirring. Never leave your spoon in the cup.

Scone etiquette: Do not slice your scone in half, sideways or from top to bottom. Simply break off a small size piece, place it on your plate and then apply, with your bread and butter knife, the jam and cream— just like a dinner roll. A fork is never used to eat a scone.

The Perfect Cup of Tea

TEA IN A BAG

Though thrifty New York merchant Thomas Sullivan invented the first 'tea bag' back in 1908, it is widely known that no such device must enter any respectable High Tea party. Tea should be brewed using loose tea and served in a teapot. Choose a teapot made from pottery, stainless steel, glass or porcelain in a size to suit the number of cups needed.

MILK AND SUGAR?

Milk is served with tea, cream is served with coffee. Originally all teacups in Europe were made from soft paste porcelain. The milk was added first to temper the cups from cracking. Once hard paste porcelain was discovered in Europe, it was no longer necessary to temper the cups. Hence, it makes more sense to add milk after the tea has brewed. The correct brewing of tea can be judged by its colour, therefore milk after is a wiser choice, but either choice is correct. For a dairy free experience, soy milk is an effective alternative. While producing a distinctly different nutty flavour, soy milk partners nicely with honey and is a preference for many.

At The Victoria Room, white and amber rough-cut cane sugar cubes will always accompany a tea or coffee order. Whether patrons decide to stir a cube through their cuppa or not is generally dependant on the size of their sweet tooth, but it is normally accepted that sugar will only be added to black or blended teas. For those who desire a sweeter herbal infusion, honey is recommended.

BLACK TEA AND BLENDING

Black teas are the most oxidised of all tea varieties, meaning that they are host to stronger flavours and aromas, as well as more caffeine. Black tea is the most popular tea variety amongst Western drinkers, though this has only been the case since the turn of the 19th century as the teas originally imported to Europe were either green or semi-oxidised.

India, Sri Lanka and China are the top tea producing countries in the world, where the unblended teas are named after the region where the leaf is grown. Indian Darjeeling is the lightest of black teas with an exceptionally fine aroma and can be enjoyed as an afternoon drink, without milk. Assam tea is full bodied with a tangibly spiced aroma, and is suitable for drinking in the morning or with milk. Sri Lanka is the third-largest producer of tea in the world and its Ceylon is a light tea with crisp citrus undertones. Chinese leaves produce black teas, which are characteristically lighter and lower in caffeine than Indian teas. The most popular Chinese teas are Keemun, Lapsang Souchong and Yunnan. Keemun is the fruitiest tea, with sweet hints of pine and flowers, whilst Lapsang Souchong is dried over a burning pipe and is thus known for its smoky qualities. Yunnan is a recommended breakfast tea and is one of the only black teas in China that suits milk.

Blending teas began around 1870 when tea merchants such as Twinings started blending different teas to achieve a stable taste. It was Twinings who first introduced the 'Earl Grey' blend of tea, created for the British Prime Minister at the time. This tea has become the favourite Chinese blend for afternoon tea with English and foreign tea connoisseurs alike. Ironically, England's favourite cuppa, English Breakfast, was first blended in New York. At The Victoria Room we serve:

English Breakfast Supreme: A traditional blend of the finest Assam and Ceylon teas producing a fully aromatic blend with lots of golden tips. A strong tea perfect with breakfast.
Earl Grey Premium: Classically scented with natural bergamot oil which gives a refreshing, lightly citrus flavour.
Prince of Wales: A blend of China black tea, a light tea with a superb and delicate aroma, making this a great blend for afternoon tea.

Queen Mary: A blend of Darjeeling and Ceylon teas, having a light amber colour and brisk aromatic flavour.

Russian Caravan: A traditional blend of China black tea, having a mild, fine aromatic and very wholesome flavour.

Scottish Breakfast: Our strongest blend! (Not for the faint hearted). A breakfast blend of African, Assam and Ceylon teas.

Assam: An Indian tea grown in the mountains of Assam, this is a strong, full bodied tea—the fine leaf (Broken Orange Pekoe) attributing to its strength. A lovely breakfast tea.

Darjeeling: Darjeeling are the rarest and most prestigious of black teas. The Victoria Room serves one of the best second flush Darjeeling teas from the Springside Estate. A very smooth liquor with a masked muscatel flavour.

China Sencha: Low in caffeine, rich in vitamin C, this is a large-leafed green tea, light and delightfully refreshing with a brisk taste. Drink with meals or as a digestive.

HERBAL AND FRUIT INFUSIONS

Herbal infusions are hot water based beverages made of anything but leaves of the tea bush. Brewed, served and drunk in exactly the same way as regular tea, herbal infusions comprise dried herbs, spices, roots, seeds or flowers that are infused in hot water. Most herbal infusions are caffeine and additive free, often with therapeutic benefits. Natural therapists regularly rely on herbal infusions to assist with the treatment of ailments such as skin disorders, allergies, circulatory problems as well as colds and flu.

Chamomile, peppermint and lemon grass are all popular single-herb choices for infusions. Chamomile is a popular remedy for the common cold, and is a soothing drink before bedtime. Peppermint infusions contain natural menthol said to ease nauseating symptoms and the minty edge is a great natural option for combating bad breath. Lemongrass is used to relieve stomach and gut problems, but can also act as a natural anti-depressant or mood enhancer. At The Victoria Room we serve:

Camomile and Spearmint

Lemongrass and Ginger

Rose Garden: A favourite at The Victoria Room: Rose buds, chamomile, lavender, hibiscus, calendula, cornflower.

Turkish Apple: Not really a tea, but beautifully sweet and tangy, just like a sweet apple. Drink hot or cold, as served in the Turkish bazaars.

Chai: The Victoria Room's hand-selected spice blend is enhanced by fresh slivers of ginger root, lush anti-oxidant enriched tea leaves and the purest honey. It's 98 per cent caffeine free and is served latte-style. Soy milk optional.

The Story of Coffee

Black as the devil, hot as hell, pure as an angel, sweet as love.
Talleyrand (1754–1838)

An amusing tale recalls the plight of an Ethiopian goatherd from Kafka who noticed that his goats became overly active after chewing on some red coffee berries. Upon observing this unusual behaviour, the goatherd tried the berries himself and found that he too was at once energised and lively. Although this may be a myth, we do know that it was common practice amongst slaves in Africa to eat the cherry-coloured flesh of the coffee berry, which is how coffee first travelled from Sudan into Yemen and Arabia, through the great port of its day, Mocha.

For decades, there was a strict policy forbidding the export of any fertile beans out of Mocha, and thus coffee could not be cultivated anywhere else. Eventually, in 1616, the Dutch managed to smuggle some live trees or beans back to Holland to secretly grow them in hidden greenhouses. The Dutch then cultivated coffee at Malabar in India, and Java, Indonesia. Today, Indonesia remains the fourth largest coffee exporter in the world.

In the 18th Century, coffee was brought to the Americas, and to this day the South American coffee industry reigns supreme. The importance of coffee in the world economy cannot be overstated. It is one of the most valuable primary products in world trade, in many years second in value only to oil as a source of foreign exchange to developing countries.

THE BREW

Brewing coffee is a fine science. While the perfect cup of coffee will depend on personal preference, according to strength and flavour, there are three essential elements that are necessary for preparing any coffee fresh filtered water, a good coffee maker and fresh quality coffee beans that have been ground correctly.

Unlike tea or cocoa, coffee lends itself readily to many different ways of making the infusion. There are several methods for brewing coffee, each significant for yielding a particular flavour. The most popular at home techniques are described below.

FRENCH PRESS/PLUNGER

The coffee plunger offers unparalleled control over the flavour of the brew due to perfect extraction time and delivery of the volatile oils often trapped in paper filters. A coffee plunger is probably the least expensive method of brewing fresh coffee. This technique is most suited to coarsely ground coffee beans.

Stove Top/Italian Style

The stove top technique creates a thick, rich brew similar to an espresso but without the crema. This method relies entirely on the natural pressure of the steam, which is produced by the water beneath a funnel holding the ground coffee beans. The resulting blend is typically an aromatic, full-bodied flavour.

Automatic Drip Coffee Maker/Filter Coffee

Drip or filter coffee is probably the simplest technique for brewing coffee in the home. Most popular with domestic coffeemakers in North America, this method was invented by a German housewife in the early 20th century. It involves using a thick paper filter that leads to a sediment-free brew, which, in turn, allows for a less bitter taste. A medium grind is normally advised for this method, though those after a stronger flavour should try using a slightly finer grind.

Espresso Machine

Espresso machines are most commonly used in commercial cafes and restaurants, but many coffee enthusiasts have invested in their own machine for the home. Espresso machines operate by forcing hot water through finely ground roast coffee beans. Coffee from such a machine is on average two to three times stronger than filter coffee, and for this reason can be used as a base for other types of milk or soy based coffees such the cappuccino or latte.

Decaf

Fortunately, decaffeinated coffee has the same anti-oxidant benefits as regular coffee. Some exciting work is showing how coffee may help reduce the risk of a number of diseases and ailments, including type 2 diabetes, Parkinson's, colon cancer, cirrhosis of the liver, gall stones, depression and more.

Sandwiches

3 cucumbers
1 bunch of radishes washed and thinly sliced
1 heaped tablespoon sea salt for pickling
zest and juice of 2 medium limes
250g (8oz/1 cup) crème fraiche
½ bunch of thinly sliced mint leaves
½ teaspoon sea salt
½ teaspoon ground white pepper
1 loaf of good quality white sliced bread

Cucumber,

MINTED RADISH AND CRÈME FRAÎCHE

Makes approximately half a loaf

Peel the skin from the cucumbers, then using the same peeler, shave cucumber into long thin ribbons.

Set shaved cucumber ribbons aside in a colander, add the thinly sliced radishes and sprinkle with the sea salt. Allow to pickle for 20 minutes.

In a medium bowl combine the lime juice and zest, crème fraiche and mint. Add sea salt and white pepper to taste.

Once the cucumber and radish are pickled place on a clean dry tea towel, roll into a log and gently ring out excess moisture.

Spread each slice of bread with a generous amount of the crème fraiche mixture and then evenly distribute cucumber and radish amongst sandwiches.

Sandwich bread together, cut off the crusts and then cut into triangles.

Tip For best results use cucumbers that are fresh, deep and rich in colour and feel full and firm to the touch. If telegraph cucumbers are unavailable substitute for Lebanese cucumbers but use 2–3 times the quantity above depending on size.

6 egg yolks
2 tablespoons lemon juice
2 teaspoons sea salt
1 teaspoon cayenne pepper
1 teaspoon smoked paprika
300g (10oz/1¹/₃ cups) butter to make 200ml (7 fl oz) clarified butter or ghee
1 teaspoon white wine vinegar
2 bunches of organic green asparagus
12 slices of good quality rye or multigrain bread

Asparagus

AND HOLLANDAISE SAUCE

Makes 6 sandwiches

Make the hollandaise sauce: In a small bowl and using a hand whisk, beat egg yokes with lemon juice, salt, cayenne pepper and paprika. Gradually beat in the clarified butter, then add white wine vinegar.

Whisk over a very low heat until mixture is slightly thickened. Take off the heat and let stand for 5–10 minutes before spreading on bread.

While the hollandaise is standing, boil a pot of lightly salted water and gently simmer.

To clean the asparagus remove the woody part at the base by gently and firmly placing your forefinger and thumb approximately 1 inch (1.5cm) from the base and breaking off. Then clean the remaining stem with a potato peeler.

Blanch the asparagus in the gently simmering water for no more than 1 minute and refresh under cold running water.

Place the asparagus spears on your chopping board, slice lengthways and then in half.

Spread each slice of bread with a generous amount of the hollandaise sauce and evenly distribute asparagus among the sandwiches.

Sandwich bread together, cut off the crusts and then cut into fingers.

Tip To make clarified butter, heat a medium saucepan until hot. Turn heat down, add 300g (10oz/1¹/₃ cups) butter and allow it to melt slowly but not brown. The milk solids will separate and fall to the bottom. Skim off the top layer of butter, leaving approximately 200ml clarified butter.

300g (10oz) piece of beef tenderloin (eye fillet)
1 tablespoon extra virgin olive oil
3 tablespoons coarsely ground black pepper
200g (7oz/1 cup) double cream
2 tablespoons creamed horseradish
2 tablespoons lemon juice
2 teaspoons sea salt
2 teaspoons white pepper
1 bunch chives chopped
3 large vine ripened tomatoes, de-seeded and finely diced
12 slices good quality country style bread

Rare Roast Beef
WITH CHIVE AND HORSERADISH CREAM

Makes 6 sandwiches

Place beef tenderloin in a bowl, drizzle with olive oil and rub with coarsely ground black pepper, until entire tenderloin is covered.

Heat a heavy-based pan and sear beef all over—1 minute on each side.

Set beef aside and allow to rest for 15–20 minutes.

Meanwhile combine double cream with creamed horseradish, lemon juice, sea salt, white pepper and chives in a bowl.

Thinly slice the seared rare beef 3–4mm ($\frac{1}{8}$ inch) thick.

Spread each slice of bread with a generous amount of the cream mixture and the rare roast beef. Top each with diced tomato.

Sandwich bread together and cut off the crusts, then cut into triangles.

Tip Horseradish cream can be quite hot for some. You can mix a little sour cream in for the more sensitive palate.

Whole Egg Mayonnaise
(Makes ½ litre, 16fl oz)

3 organic free-range egg yolks
½ teaspoon seasalt
juice of 1 lemon
1 teaspoon white wine vinegar
350ml (12fl oz/1¼ cups)
sunflower oil
white pepper to taste

6 organic free-range eggs
1 heaped teaspoon golden Ras el Hanout (North African spice mix)
125ml (4 fl oz/½ cup) whole egg mayonnaise
1 teaspoon sea salt (adding more if necessary)
coriander to garnish
12 slices good quality white bread

A Twist on
CLASSIC CURRIED EGG

Makes 6 sandwiches

To make the mayonnaise: whisk yolks, salt, lemon and vinegar for 1 minute until smooth.

Gradually beat in the oil adding the first few tablespoons one at a time and whisking well after each addition. Once a third of the oil has been added, the rest can be added in a steady stream beating all the while.

Taste for seasoning and adjust with salt and white pepper.

Gently place eggs in a saucepan, fill with water and bring to a gentle boil. Take off heat and allow to cool in pan for 10 minutes. Then run under cold running water. Peel eggs and then crush using a potato masher or a fork.

Sprinkle golden Ras el Hanout over the crushed eggs and mix in the mayonnaise and sea salt.

Spread each slice of bread with a generous amount of the egg mixture, distributing evenly. Top each with some baby coriander, sandwich bread together and cut off the crusts, then cut into triangles.

Tip Ras el Hanout is a mixture of nearly 30 different spices. The composition varies from one spice merchant to another and is sold in ground form or with the spices left whole. It can be purchased from all good spice merchants and Middle Eastern stores. If Ras el Hanout is unavailable curry powder can be used instead.

Filling

1 organic free-range chicken
1 carrot, peeled and roughly
chopped
1 brown onion, cut into eighths
1 stick of celery, roughly chopped
1 bay leaf
black peppercorns
rind of 1 lemon
1 bunch thyme
1 bunch picked chopped parsley
(saving stalks for stock)
500g (17.5 fl oz/1½ cups) aioli
1 bunch chopped chives
1 bunch fresh basil, chopped
1 bunch fresh mint, chopped
12 slices soft fluffy white bread

Aioli (makes ½ litre, 16fl oz)

5 cloves of garlic
1 teaspoon seasalt
3 organic free-range egg yolks
1 teaspoon Dijon mustard
1 teaspoon white wine vinegar
juice of 1 lemon
500ml (17oz/2 cups) sunflower oil
sea salt and pepper to taste

Chicken
AND WILD HERBS

Makes 6 sandwiches

Place washed chicken in a large saucepan and cover with water. Add carrot, onion, celery, bay leaf, peppercorns, lemon rind, thyme and parsley stalks. Bring to a gentle boil and simmer for 35–45 minutes until chicken is falling off the bone.

Remove chicken and allow it to cool. Hand shred the meat.

While the chicken is cooling, make the aioli. In a food processor or mortar and pestle process or grind the garlic with the salt to form a paste. Transfer to a bowl and whisk in the yolks, mustard, vinegar and lemon juice to form a smooth paste.

Start gradually adding the oil, a few teaspoons at a time while constantly whisking, and then the rest can be added in a steady stream beating all the while until all the oil has been added. Taste for seasoning and adjust with salt and white pepper.

Combine aioli, chicken and herbs in a bowl. Spread each slice of bread with a generous amount of the chicken mixture distributing evenly. Sandwich bread together, cut off the crusts and then cut into triangles.

Tip Reserve chicken stock and freeze in 1 litre bags for future use. Substitute the whole chicken with thigh fillet or Maryland for ease of preparation.

500g (17.5oz/2 cups) cream cheese
at room temperature
juice and zest of 1 lemon
2 teaspoon sea salt
1 teaspoon white pepper
150g (5oz/1 cup) chopped baby
capers
1 small Spanish onion, finely diced
1 bunch chives, chopped
350g (11½oz) smoked salmon
1 bunch washed rocket
12 slices dark rye bread

Smoked Salmon,
ROCKET, LEMON AND CAPERS

Makes 6 sandwiches

In a bowl cream together with an electric or hand beater the cream cheese, lemon zest, juice, sea salt and pepper to a whipped cream consistency. Fold in the capers, onion and chives.

Spread each slice of bread with a generous amount of the cream cheese mixture, distributing evenly, then the smoked salmon and rocket. Sandwich bread together, cut off the crusts and then cut into triangles.

Tip We like to use dark rye for this recipe, but sourdough is a good alternative. The cream cheese mix also works in a potato salad with flaked smoked salmon or trout and a touch of sour cream.

zest and juice of 2 limes
sea salt and freshly ground black
pepper to taste
¼ teaspoon freshly ground cumin
125 ml (4 fl oz/½ cup) whole egg
mayonnaise (see page 19)
1 loaf soft white pane di casa
(Italian bread)
800g (28oz) lobster tail meat
cooked and sliced
2 cucumbers peeled and shaved
into ribbons
1 bunch picked coriander

Lobster Tail

WITH LIME AIOLI AND FRESH CORIANDER

Serves 6

Combine lime zest, juice, salt and pepper and cumin in a bowl with the mayonnaise to make the lime aioli.

Spread each slice of bread with a generous amount of the lime aioli then evenly distribute lobster meat, cucumber and coriander and season to taste. Sandwich bread together, cut off the crusts and then cut into triangles or squares.

Tip Your local fishmonger should have lobster meat, whatever the season. Buy a cooked whole lobster (fresh or frozen) and with a large cook's knife separate the head from the tail. Lay the tail on your cutting board belly up and carefully cut through the shell lengthways. You should easily be able to remove the meat from there. Alternatively, you can buy just the frozen lobster tails, from which you can remove the meat.

2 organic free-range eggs
125ml (4fl oz/½ cup) whole egg
mayonnaise (see page 19)
40g (1.5oz/¼ cup) cornichons,
chopped
40g (1.5oz/¼ cup) baby capers,
chopped
40g (1.5oz/¼ cup) finely diced
tomato, deseeded
1 tablespoon Italian (flat leaf)
parsley, chopped
1 tablespoon fresh tarragon,
chopped
sea salt and pepper to taste
12 slices light rye or wholemeal
bread
1 head of baby cos washed and
patted dry
1 smoked trout flaked and deboned

Smoked Trout
WITH LETTUCE AND DILL GREBECHE

Makes 6 sandwiches

Place eggs in a saucepan, fill with water and bring to a gentle boil. Take off heat and allow to cool in pan for 10 minutes then run under cold running water. Peel eggs and then crush using a potato masher or a fork, don't over mash.

In a separate bowl combine mayonnaise, cornichons, capers, tomato, parsley, tarragon and season to taste. Then add the crushed egg.

Spread each slice of bread with a generous amount of the grebeche, distributing evenly the baby cos and flaked trout. Sandwich bread together, cut off the crusts and then cut into triangles or fingers.

Tip Cornichons is the French name for pickled gherkins. Cooked salmon fillet can be substituted for the smoked trout if desired.

300g (10oz/1¹/₃ cups) goats cheese
200g (7oz/1 cup) cream cheese at
room temperature
zest and juice of 1 lemon
1 teaspoon ground white pepper
1 teaspoon sea salt
150g (5oz/1¹/₃ cup) diced celery
150g (5oz/1¹/₃) cup roasted
walnuts, chopped
12 slices soft multigrain bread
1 cup firmly packed watercress

Watercress, Celery
WALNUTS AND GOATS CHEESE

Makes 6 sandwiches

Mix goats cheese, cream cheese, lemon juice and zest and seasoning until well combined. Then add celery and walnuts.

Spread each slice of bread with a generous amount of the goat's cheese mixture, evenly distributing the watercress. Sandwich bread together, cut off the crusts and then cut into triangles.

Tip For best results use the centre stalks of the celery and young leaves.

Scones

800g (28oz/5½ cups) self-raising flour
½ teaspoon baking powder
pinch of salt
170g (5oz/ ¾ cup) unsalted butter, chopped and chilled
150g (5oz/¾ cup) castor sugar
zest of 1 lemon
300ml (10 fl oz) milk
1 tablespoon vanilla essence
extra milk for glazing

The Original
VICTORIA ROOM SCONE

Makes 18 scones

Preheat the oven to 180°C (350°F). Line a large baking tray with greaseproof paper.

Sift together flour and baking powder, then add salt. Using fingertips rub in chilled butter. Add sugar and lemon zest and rub further until mixture resembles breadcrumbs.

Then make a well in the centre of the flour mixture and slowly pour in the milk with the vanilla. Working quickly, take the flour into the centre using a fork to make a soft dough. Form into a soft ball with floured hands.

Turn out the dough onto a floured board. Give it a few turns and gently roll out with a floured rolling pin to a 2½ cm (1 in) thickness.

Cut into rounds with a 5cm (2 in) scone cutter making sure not to twist the cutter.

Place the scones on the prepared tray approximately 2½ cm (1 in) apart and brush with millk to glaze. Bake for 15–18 minutes or until golden. Then turn out onto a wire rack to cool slightly.

Serve with your favourite jam or conserve (see Conserves section).

Tip The secret to The Victoria Room's famous scone recipe is to place the lemon zest in with the sugar.

800g (28oz/5½ cups) self-raising
flour
1 teaspoon cinnamon
½ teaspoon baking powder
pinch of salt
150g (5oz/⅔ cup) unsalted butter,
chopped and chilled
150g (5oz/¾ cup) castor sugar
zest of 4 oranges
300ml (10fl oz) milk
1 tablespoon vanilla essence
300g (10oz/1⅓ cups) dates,
chopped
milk for glazing
extra cinnamon for dusting

Date Scones

Makes 18

Preheat the oven to 180°C (350°F). Line a flat baking tray with
greaseproof paper.

Sift together flour, cinnamon and baking powder, and then add salt.
Using fingertips, rub in chilled butter. Then add sugar and orange
zest and rub further until mixture resembles breadcrumbs.

Then make a well in the centre of the flour mixture and slowly pour
in the milk with the vanilla. Working quickly, take the flour into the
centre using a fork to make a soft dough. Form into a soft ball with
floured hands.

Turn out the dough onto a floured board, add the dates, give it a few
turns and gently roll out with a floured rolling pin to a 2½ cm (1 in)
thickness.

Cut into rounds with a 5cm (2 in) scone cutter making sure not to
twist the cutter.

Place the scones on the prepared tray approximately 2½ cm (1 in)
apart, brush with milk to glaze and dust with extra cinnamon and
bake for 15–18 minutes or until golden. Then turn out onto a wire
rack to cool slightly.

Serve with your favourite jam or conserve (See Conserves section).

320g (11oz/2 cups) gluten free flour sifted
3 teaspoons baking powder
¼ teaspoon salt
120g (4oz/½ cup) margarine
2 tablespoons raw sugar
zest of 1 orange
1 vanilla bean scraped
175ml (6 fl oz/¾ cup) soymilk
120g (4oz/½ cup) chopped dates (optional)
soy milk for glazing

Gluten Free Scones

Makes 8 scones

Preheat the oven to 170°C (325°F). Line a flat baking tray with greaseproof paper.

Sift together flour and baking powder, and then add salt.

Cream together margarine and sugar until light and fluffy.

Add orange zest, vanilla and the flour mixture and milk alternatively. Mix through the dates.

Turn out the dough onto a floured board. Give it a few turns and gently roll out with a floured rolling pin to a 2½ cm (1 in) thickness.

Cut into rounds with a 5cm (2 in) scone cutter making sure not to twist the cutter.

Place the scones on the prepared tray approximately 2½ cm (1 in) apart, brush with extra milk to glaze and bake for 7 minutes, then turn over and bake for a further 7 minutes or until golden. Then turn out onto a wire rack to cool slightly.

Serve with your favourite jam or conserve (see Conserves section).

Tip Gluten free flour can be purchased from most supermarkets or health food stores.

450g (15oz/2¾ cups) self-raising
flour sifted
½ teaspoon baking powder
pinch of salt
150g (5oz/⅔ cup) unsalted diced
and chilled butter
100g (3½oz/½ cup) castor sugar
150g (5oz) glacé cherries roughly
chopped
1 organic free-range egg lightly
beaten
zest of 1 lemon
2–3 drops almond essence
180–200ml (6–7 fl oz/¾ cup) milk
flaked almonds to garnish

Cherry and Almond

SCONES

Makes 16 scones

Preheat the oven to 180°C (350°F). Line a flat baking tray with
greaseproof paper.

Sift together flour and baking powder, and then add salt. Using
fingertips rub in chilled butter. Then add sugar, cherries, egg, lemon
zest and almond essence and milk to give a soft but not too sticky
dough. Knead until smooth.

After giving the dough a few turns, gently roll out with a floured
rolling pin to a 2½ cm (1 in) thickness.

Cut into rounds with a 5cm (2 in) scone cutter making sure not to
twist the cutter.

Place the scones on the prepared tray approximately 2½ cm (1 in)
apart, brush with milk to glaze and garnish with the flaked almonds
and bake for 15–18 minutes or until golden. Then turn out onto a
wire rack to cool slightly.

Serve with Chantilly cream (see recipe on page 58) or your favourite
jam or conserve (see Conserves section).

640–800g (22–28oz/4–5 cups)
self-raising flour
2 teaspoons baking soda
1 teaspoon grated nutmeg
2 teaspoon ground cinnamon
1½ teaspoons salt
120g (4oz/½ cup) butter
200g (7oz/1 cup) castor sugar
125ml (4 fl oz/½ cup) sour cream
2 organic free-range eggs
2 cups roasted butternut pumpkin
at room temperature, mashed
1 teaspoon fresh ginger, grated
milk for glazing

Pumpkin and Ginger

SCONE

Makes 18–20 scones

Preheat the oven to 180°C (350°F). Line a flat baking tray with greaseproof paper.

Sift together flour, baking soda, nutmeg, cinnamon and salt. Using fingertips, rub in chilled butter. Then add sugar and rub further until mixture resembles breadcrumbs.

Lightly whisk together the sour cream and eggs.

Then make a well in the centre of the flour mixture and slowly pour in the sour cream mixture. Then add the mashed pumpkin and the grated ginger. Working quickly, take the flour into the centre using a fork to make a soft dough. Form into a soft ball with floured hands.

Turn out the dough on a floured board. Give it a few turns and gently roll out with a floured rolling pin to a 2½ cm (1 in) thickness.

Cut into rounds with a 5cm (2 in) scone cutter making sure not to twist the cutter.

Place the scones on the prepared tray approximately 2½ cm (1 in) apart, brush with milk to glaze and bake for 15–20 minutes or until golden. Then turn out onto a wire rack to cool slightly.

Serve with a soft feta cheese.

Tip Begin by using 4 cups of self-raising flour. If you find the dough is too moist and sticking to the surface of the bacon or bowl, add more flour as needed.

640g (22oz/4 cups) self-raising flour
1 teaspoon salt
½ teaspoon white pepper
1 teaspoon smoky paprika
230g (7oz/1 cup) diced cold unsalted butter
300g (10oz/1⅓ cups) sour cream
2 organic free-range eggs
100g (3½oz/½ cup) castor sugar
1 bunch chives, sliced

Chive Scones

WITH SOUR CREAM

Makes 16 scones

Preheat the oven to 180°C (350°F). Line a large baking tray with greaseproof paper.

Sift together flour, salt, pepper and paprika. Using fingertips rub in chilled butter. Then add sugar and chives and rub further until mixture resembles breadcrumbs.

Lightly whisk together the sour cream and eggs.

Then make a well in the centre of the flour mixture and slowly pour in the cream mixture. Working quickly, take the flour into the centre using a fork to make a soft dough. Form into a soft ball with floured hands.

Turn out the dough on a floured board. Give it a few turns and gently roll out with a floured rolling pin to a 2½ cm (1 in) thickness.

Cut into rounds with a 5cm (2 in) scone cutter making sure not to twist the cutter.

Place the scones on the prepared tray approximately 2½ cm (1 in) apart and bake for 15–18 minutes or until golden. Then turn out onto a wire rack to cool slightly.

Serve with smoked salmon, lemon, rocket and capers or your favourite cheese.

Tip This scone is good simply with cold smoked salmon, a dollop of sour cream and freshly chopped chives. Perfect for a late Sunday breakfast.

800g (28oz/5 cups) self-raising flour
1 teaspoon salt
230g (7oz/1 cup) diced cold unsalted butter
175g (6oz/¾ cup) castor sugar
3 lemons zested and juiced
100g (3½oz/½ cup) currants
150g (5oz/1 cup) pistachios—half roughly chopped, half finely chopped
250ml (8.5fl oz/1 cup) milk
2 organic free-range eggs
1 teaspoon vanilla

Lemon, Pistachio
AND CURRANT SCONES

Makes 18 scones

Preheat the oven to 180°C (350°F). Line a large baking tray with greaseproof paper.

Sift together flour and salt. Using fingertips rub in chilled butter. Then add sugar and lemon zest and rub further until mixture resembles breadcrumbs. Then mix in currants and pistachios.

Lightly whisk together the milk, eggs, vanilla and lemon juice.

Then make a well in the centre of the flour mixture and slowly pour in the milk mixture. Working quickly, take the flour into the centre using a fork to make a soft dough. Form into a soft ball with floured hands.

Turn out the dough on a floured board. Give it a few turns and gently roll out with a floured rolling pin to a 2½ cm (1 in) thickness.

Cut into rounds with a 5cm (2 in) scone cutter making sure not to twist the cutter.

Place the scones on the prepared tray approximately 2½ cm (1 in) apart and bake for 15–18 minutes or until golden. Then turn out onto a wire rack to cool slightly.

Serve with your favourite jam or conserve (see Conserves section).

Tip This recipe is a variation on an Italian cake Joe enjoyed when he was growing up. These scones are delicious with mascarpone.

950g (33.5oz/6 cups) self-raising
flour
½ teaspoon baking powder
pinch of salt
150g (5oz/¾ cup) unsalted butter
chopped and chilled
150g (5oz/¾ cup) castor sugar
zest of 1 lemon
500g (17.5oz/3 cups) white
chocolate chopped
1 tablespoon vanilla essence
200ml (6.7fl oz) milk
200ml (6.7fl oz) buttermilk

White Chocolate

SCONES

Makes 24

Preheat the oven to 180°C (350°F). Line a flat baking tray with
greaseproof paper.

Sift together flour, baking powder and salt. Using fingertips rub
in chilled butter. Then add sugar and lemon zest and rub further
until mixture resembles breadcrumbs. Then mix in chopped white
chocolate.

Lightly whisk together the milk, buttermilk, eggs and vanilla.

Then make a well in the centre of the flour mixture and slowly pour
in the milk mixture. Working quickly, take the flour into the centre
using a fork to make a soft dough. Form into a soft ball with floured
hands.

Turn out the dough on a floured board. Give it a few turns and
gently roll out with a floured rolling pin to a 2½ cm (1 in) thickness.

Cut into rounds with a 5cm (2 in) scone cutter making sure not to
twist the cutter.

Place the scones on the prepared tray approximately 2½ cm (1 in)
apart and bake for 18–22 minutes or until golden. Then turn out
onto a wire rack to cool slightly.

Serve with your favourite jam or conserve (see Conserves section).

*Tip To keep scones soft and fluffy place a dry tea towel over the scones as
soon as they are removed from the oven.*

Cupcakes

250ml (8 fl oz/1 cup) milk
1 vanilla bean cut lengthways
80g (2½oz/½ cup) butter chopped
at room temperature
200g (7oz/1 cup) castor sugar
1 organic free-range egg
310g (11oz/2½ cups) plain flour
2 teaspoons baking powder
1 teaspoon salt
1 teaspoon vanilla essence
24 mini paper cupcake cases

Soft Pink Icing
60g (3oz) unsalted butter, at room
temperature, chopped
170g (6oz/1¼ cup) icing sugar
1 tablespoon milk
3 drops pink food colouring

Vanilla Bean Cupcakes
WITH SOFT PINK ICING

Makes 24 mini cupcakes

Preheat oven to 170°C (325°F). Line 24-hole mini muffin tin with paper cupcake cases.

In a small saucepan heat the milk and vanilla bean together until the milk just boils. Remove from the heat and allow to cool for 1 hour. Remove the vanilla bean and scrape the seeds, adding to the milk, and set aside discarding the remaining vanilla pod.

Cream together the butter and sugar until light and fluffy. Add the egg and vanilla essence and beat well. In a separate bowl sift the flour and baking powder together then add the salt. Alternately add the flour mixture and milk mixture to the butter mixture until well combined.

Divide batter evenly amongst the 24-hole mini muffin tin. Bake for 12–15 minutes until golden and the tops spring back lightly to the touch. Turn out onto a wire rack to cool completely.

While cakes are cooling beat together the ingredients for the icing. Once cakes are completely cooled top with the icing.

Tip These are always a hit at children's parties too. A fun party activity is to let your young guests decorate the cupcakes. Offer different coloured icings, some interesting lollies and sprinkles for decoration. A guaranteed winner!

185ml (6.5oz/¾ cup) milk
1 vanilla bean cut lengthways
2 tablespoons loose leaf chai tea
80g (2½oz/½ cup) butter chopped
at room temperature
200g (7oz/1 cup) castor sugar
1 organic free–range egg
380g (13oz/3 cups) plain flour
2 teaspoons baking powder
1 teaspoon salt
24 mini paper cupcake cases

Lime Mascarpone Icing
120g (4oz/½ cup) mascarpone
250g (8oz/1 cup) icing sugar
zest and juice of 2 limes

Chai Cupcakes
WITH LIME MASCARPONE

Makes 24 mini cupcakes

Preheat oven to 170°C (325°F). Line 24-hole muffin tin with paper cupcake cases.

In a small saucepan heat the milk, vanilla bean and chai tea together until the milk just boils. Remove from the heat and allow to cool for 1 hour. Remove the vanilla bean and strain to remove the chai tea. Scrape the vanilla bean adding the seeds to the strained milk and set aside discarding the remaining vanilla pod.

With an electric beater, cream together the butter and sugar until pale and fluffy. Add the egg and beat well. In a separate bowl sift the flour and baking powder together then add the salt. Add the flour mixture and milk mixture to the butter mixture a little at a time folding through until well combined.

Divide batter evenly amongst the 24-hole muffin tin. Bake for 12–15 minutes until golden and spring back lightly to the touch. Turn out onto a wire rack to cool completely.

While cakes are cooling whisk together the ingredients for the icing. Once cakes are completely cooled top with the icing.

Tip We use fresh spices in our chai, however, chai can come in varying forms, such as powder, leaves or syrup. For this recipe we recommend loose leaf chai, available at all major supermarkets.

Cupcakes

125g (4oz) butter at room
temperature, diced
100g (3½oz/½ cup) white
chocolate chopped
200g (7oz/1 cup) castor sugar
125ml (4fl oz/½ cup) milk
1 organic free-range egg lightly
beaten
120g (4oz/¾ cup) plain flour
80g (2½oz/½ cup) self-raising
flour
1 teaspoon vanilla bean paste (or
extract if paste is not available)
silver cachous to garnish
12 paper cupcake cases

White Chocolate Ganache

360g (12oz/1¾ cups) white
chocolate chopped
125ml (4fl oz/½ cup) thickened
cream
2–3 drops pink food colouring, or
any other colour

White Chocolate Cupcakes
WITH WHITE CHOCOLATE GANACHE

Makes 12 cupcakes

Preheat oven to 160°C (310°F). Line 12-hole muffin tin with paper cupcake cases.

Combine butter, chocolate, sugar and milk in a medium saucepan stirring over low heat until ingredients have combined and mixture is smooth. Transfer to a heatproof bowl and allow to cool slightly.

Once mixture has slightly cooled, whisk in the egg and sifted flours until just combined. Then add the vanilla bean paste.

Divide mixture evenly amongst 12 paper cupcake cases and bake for 30 minutes until golden and cakes are firm to the touch.

Turn out onto a wire rack and allow to cool completely.

To make the white chocolate icing, combine chocolate and cream in a heatproof bowl over a bain marie stirring until the mixture is smooth. Place icing into the refrigerator for 1–1½ hours until mixture is spreadable. Add food colouring and mix to combine.

Using a flat spatula spread the cupcakes with the icing and garnish with the silver cachous.

Tip Be sure to use a good quality white chocolate, for example fine Belgian chocolate, as it gives a richer creamier flavour.

Cupcakes

120g (4oz/½ cup) butter chopped
at room temperature
65g (2oz/⅓ cup) castor sugar
½ teaspoon coconut essence
1 organic free-range egg
130g (4oz/1 cup) self-raising flour
30g (1oz/⅓ cup) desiccated
coconut
50g (¾oz/½ cup) toasted desiccated
coconut to garnish
(see tip below)
65 ml (2 fl oz/¼ cup) milk
18 mini paper cupcake cases

Icing

60g (2oz) unsalted butter chopped
at room temperature
160g (6oz/1 cup) icing sugar
1 tablespoon milk

Coconut Cupcakes
WITH CREAMY COCONUT ICING

Makes 18 mini cupcakes

Preheat oven to 180°C (350°F). Grease a 18-hole mini-muffin tin.

With an electric beater, cream together butter, sugar and coconut essence in a bowl it is pale and fluffy. Add the egg and beat to combine.

In a separate bowl sift the flour and then add the dessicated coconut. Stir the flour and coconut into the butter mixture alternately with the milk until just combined.

Divide mixture amongst the 18-hole mini muffin tin.

Bake for 12–15 minutes until golden and spring back lightly to the touch. Allow to cool slightly and then turn out onto a wire rack to cool completely.

While the cakes are cooling combine the icing ingredients in a bowl and beat until smooth. Spread the icing over the cool cakes and garnish with the toasted desiccated coconut.

Tip For perfectly roasted desiccated coconut, cook over low heat in a dry frypan, stirring until golden brown. Then remove from the pan to prevent further browning.

700g (24.6oz) good quality dark chocolate, chopped
200g (7oz/1 cup) Rose Turkish delight squares, chopped into quarters
250g (8oz/1 cup) raspberry and vanilla marshmallows, chopped into quarters
100g (3½oz/½ cup) roasted hazelnuts
100g (3½oz/½ cup) roasted pistachio nuts
100g (3½oz/½ cup) roasted almonds
24–30 mini paper cupcake cases

Mini Rocky Road

CUPCAKES

Makes 24–30 mini cupcakes

Stir chocolate in a medium heatproof bowl over a medium saucepan of simmering water until smooth.

While chocolate is melting, combine all the other ingredients in a separate bowl.

Once chocolate has melted pour it over the other ingredients and stir to combine.

Pour mixture into 24–30 pre-prepared mini-muffin tins lined with paper cupcake cases. Place in the refrigerator to set for approximately 30–40 minutes.

Tip To temper the chocolate use the following method. Place the chocolate in a heatproof bowl over the warm water in the bain marie for 5–10 seconds, remove it and stir, and repeat, until the temperature reaches 31 degrees (30 for milk and white chocolate). Do not leave the chocolate over the hot water, or allow it to exceed 33 degrees. To use tempered chocolate, you must keep it warm but not hot, ideally in the 29–31 degree range (30 degrees for milk and white chocolate). You can either keep it over a pan of warm (but not simmering) water, stirring occasionally, or try placing it on an electric heating pad set to 'low'. Whichever method you choose, it's important to stir often so that the chocolate remains a uniform temperature throughout.

425g (15oz/1½ cups) can pitted cherries in syrup
165g (6oz) butter roughly chopped at room temperature
100g (3½oz/½ cup) good quality dark cooking chocolate roughly chopped
100g (3½oz/½ cup) dark eating chocolate
215g (7.5oz/1⅓ cups) castor sugar
75ml (2.5 fl oz/¼ cup) cherry brandy plus 2 teaspoon set aside
170g (2.5oz/1 cup) plain flour
2 tablespoons self-raising flour
2 tablespoons cocoa powder
1 organic free-range egg
12 paper cupcake cases
165ml (7 fl oz/⅔ cup) thickened cream, whipped
dark chocolate for garnish

Black Forest
CUPCAKES

Makes 12 cupcakes

Preheat oven to 170°C/150°C. Line a 12-hole muffin tin with paper cases.

Drain the cherries reserving the syrup. In a blender or food processor, process 130g (4¼oz) cherries with 125ml (4fl oz/½ cup) of the reserved syrup until smooth. Slice the remaining cherries in half and set aside. Discard the remaining syrup.

Place butter, chocolate, sugar, brandy and cherry puree in a small saucepan stirring to combine over low heat until chocolate has melted. Place mixture in a medium bowl to cool.

Once mixture has cooled, lightly whisk in sifted flours and cocoa. Then add the egg. Divide mixture evenly between the 12-holed muffin tin.

Bake for 45 minutes. Once cooked and firm to the touch remove from the oven and allow cooling before turning out onto a wire rack to completely cool.

Combine whipped cream and remaining cherry brandy. Spread the cream mixture evenly over the completely cooled cakes. Top with the remaining cherry halves.

Using a peeler or a grater, grate the remaining chocolate and sprinkle over the cakes to garnish.

Tip If you don't happen to have cherry brandy, you can use any other quality brandy.

Conserves

500ml (17 fl oz/2 cups) thickened
cream
1 vanilla bean scraped
50g (1.7oz/¼ cup) pure icing
sugar sifted

Chantilly Cream

Makes enough for 18 scones

Combine all ingredients in a large bowl and using an electric mixer,
beat until thick and mixture resembles whipped cream.

350g (12.3oz) cream cheese at
room temperature
4 large passionfruits with pulp
removed and strained and set aside
100g (3.5oz/½ cup) icing sugar
sifted

Passion Fruit Cream

Makes enough for 18 scones

Combine all ingredients in a large bowl and whisk vigorously until
smooth.
Then add the reserved passionfruit pulp and stir through the cream
mixture.

*Tip Serve with your favourite scone or as a side with a slice of your
favourite cake.*

250g (8oz/1 cup) strawberries washed, cleaned and tops removed
170g (1 cup) icing sugar sifted
2 teaspoons strawberry liqueur or Cointreau
450g (15.8oz) cream cheese at room temperature

Strawberry Cream

Makes enough for 24 scones

Using a stick blender blitz together strawberries and icing sugar until smooth.

Then add the liqueur and mix.

Combine with cream cheese in a large bowl and whisk vigorously.

Tip Serve with Angel Cake (see page 78).

4 organic free-range egg yolks
100g (3½oz/½ cup) castor sugar
zest of 2 lemons finely chopped
125ml (4oz/½ cup) lemon juice
180g (6.3oz) cold, diced, unsalted
butter

Lemon Curd

Makes approximately 1¾ cups

Whisk together egg yolks, sugar, lemon juice and zest in a saucepan.

Place on a medium heat stirring constantly until the mixture is thick enough to coat the back of a wooden spoon (about 5–7 minutes) then remove saucepan from heat.

Add the butter one piece at a time and stir until the consistency is smooth.

Transfer to a heatproof bowl and lay a sheet of plastic wrap or greaseproof paper directly onto the surface of the curd to avoid a skin forming. Let cool and refrigerate until firm and chilled— approximately 1 hour.

Store refrigerated in an airtight container.

Tip To store, place in an airtight container and refrigerate. It should last up to 3 weeks.

1.5kg (3lb) pumpkin
850g (30oz/5¼ cups) castor sugar
150ml (5fl oz/²/₃ cup) water
juice of 5 lemons
3 cinnamon sticks
3 tablespoons golden syrup

Pumpkin
AND CINNAMON JAM

Makes approximately 1.25 litres (2 pints)

Peel and clean the pumpkin removing all seeds and cut into medium sized cubes.

In a heavy-based saucepan add all ingredients and stir over low heat until sugar is dissolved.

Increase heat to high and bring mixture to the boil. Then turn down and cook for 30–60 minutes stirring often.

Allow to cool and enjoy.

230g (7oz/1 cup) unsalted butter
at room temperature
1 vanilla bean scraped
2–3 drops pink food colouring
½ teaspoon rose water
fresh washed organic rose petals to
garnish

Rose Butter

Makes approximately 1 cup

Combine butter, vanilla, food colouring and rosewater in a bowl and
whip until butter is light and pale and air has been incorporated.

*Tip Serve with the Original VR Scone and garnish with fresh washed
organic rose petals for a tantalising treat.*

5 oranges thinly sliced including the peel
1 teaspoon salt
4.5 litres (155 fl oz) water
castor sugar

Italian Style
ORANGE MARMALADE

Makes 2.5 kg (5lb) marmalade

Thinly slice the fruit making sure to remove the pips and central membrane.

Simmer fruit, salt and water until peel is soft and easily squashed.

Transfer to a stainless steel bowl and allow to rest overnight.

Once rested, measure the amount of pulp you have and add the same quantity of castor sugar and water to fruit (for example 1 cup fruit= 1 cup sugar=1 cup water) in a large saucepan. Return to the boil and cook for 25–30 minutes until the fruit mixture is at the setting or jelly stage.

Whilst mixture is still warm ladle marmalade into hot, sterilised jars.

Tip To sterilise jars place in a steamer open side down to avoid burning yourself when you remove them. Fill the jars 1 cm from the top and place lids on the jars while the mixture is still hot. As the jam cools, a vacuum forms which creates an air tight seal. This procedure can be used for all jam recipes.

2 kg (4lb) cumquats washed,
quartered and deseeded
600g (21oz/3¾ cups) castor sugar
250ml (8fl oz/1 cup) water
500ml (1lb/2 cups) orange juice
juice of 1 lemon
200g (7oz) Golden Syrup
3 cloves
1 cinnamon stick

Cumquat Marmalade

Makes approximately 1.25 litres (2 pints)

Combine all ingredients in a saucepan and bring to a gentle simmer. Cook down until desired consistency is reached, approximately 1–2 hours.

See page 65 for tips on sterilising and storing in jars.

2 kg (4lb) organic strawberries,
washed, cleaned and tops removed
and then cut in half
640g (22.5oz/4 cups) castor sugar
1 vanilla bean split lengthways
juice of 4 lemons

Organic
STRAWBERRY JAM

Makes approximately 1.25 litres (2 pints)

In a heavy-based saucepan add all ingredients and stir over low heat until sugar is dissolved.

Increase heat to high and bring mixture to the boil. Then turn down and cook for 20–30 minutes stirring often.

Allow to cool.

See page 65 for tips on sterilising and storing in jars.

500g (1lb) strawberries,
blueberries, raspberries
480g (16.9oz/3 cups) castor sugar
juice of 4 lemons
1 cinnamon stick
1 vanilla bean split lengthways

Triple Berry Jam

Makes 750mls (1½ pints)

In a heavy-based saucepan add all ingredients and stir over low heat until sugar is dissolved.

Increase heat to high and bring mixture to the boil. Then turn down and cook for 30–60 minutes stirring often.

Allow to cool.

See page 65 for tips on sterilising and storing in jars.

800g (28.2oz) apples, peeled and
diced into large pieces (pink lady
apples are best)
750g (26.4oz) rhubarb, peeled and
cut into 5cm (2 in) lengths
1 kg (35.2oz/6¼ cups) castor sugar
250ml (8.5 fl oz/1 cup) water
juice of 2 lemons
1 cinnamon stick

Apple, Rhubarb Jam

Makes approximately 1.5 litres (2½ pints)

In a heavy based saucepan add pumpkin, sugar and water and boil until soft removing any foam that forms on the surface. Cook until two-thirds of the original mix remains.

Then add remaining ingredients to the saucepan and cook until mix reduces another third.

Allow to cool and remove cinnamon stick.

See page 65 for tips on sterilising and storing in jars.

500ml (17 fl oz/2 cups) lychee
juice
500ml (17 fl oz/2 cups) water
80g (2½oz/½ cup) castor sugar
¼ teaspoon pink food colouring
30g (1oz) powdered gelatin
1 vanilla bean, split and scraped
of seeds

Rose Jelly Cups

Serves 4–6

In a small saucepan, whisk the lychee juice, water, sugar and food colouring until the sugar is dissolved.

Place on a medium heat and add the vanilla bean, stirring well.

Bring mix to a simmer and remove from the heat.

Allow it to cool for 15 minutes before adding gelatin.

Stir through the gelatin until it is well dissolved and then pour into your moulds.

Refrigerate for 1 hour and serve.

Cakes, Muffins
and Slices

230g (7oz/1 cup) unsalted butter
at room temperature
50g (1¾oz/¼ cup) brown sugar
100g (3½oz/½ cup) castor sugar
1 vanilla bean scraped
zest from 2 lemons
3 organic free-range eggs
125ml (4 fl oz/½ cup) buttermilk
300ml (10fl oz) thick creamy
yoghurt
160g (5.6oz/1¼ cup) plain flour
sifted
160g (5.6oz/1¼ cup) self-raising
flour sifted
1 teaspoon baking powder
½ teaspoon cinnamon

Apple Filling and Topping
3 large apples (granny smith is
best)
juice from 2 lemons
50g (1¾oz/¼ cup) brown sugar
½ teaspoon cinnamon

Spiced Apple
TEA CAKE

Serves 10–12

Preheat the oven to 180°C (350°F). Grease and line a 20cm (8 in) loaf tin.

Peel and slice the apples and macerate in the lemon juice, sugar and cinnamon and set aside while making the cake.

With an electric mixer, cream together butter, sugars, scraped vanilla bean and lemon zest until light and fluffy.

Add eggs one at a time beating after each addition.

Whisk together the buttermilk and yoghurt. In a separate bowl combine the flours, baking powder and cinnamon.

Alternate mixing the flour mixture and yoghurt mixture into the egg mixture until smooth and well combined.

Pour half of the cake batter into the prepared tin, add half the apple mixture, and then pour the remainder of the cake batter over the top to cover. Top the cake with the remaining apples and press lightly 5mm (¼ in) deep.

Bake for 1 hour or until golden and the top springs back lightly to the touch.

Tip For best results rotate every 15 minutes and check every 5 minutes after 45 minutes to avoid burning. If browning too quickly turn oven down to 160°C (310°F) after 45 minutes.

Custard

1 tablespoon custard powder
1 tablespoon castor sugar
150ml (5.1 fl oz/⅔ cup) milk
¼ teaspoon vanilla extract

Tea Cakes

120g (4oz/½ cup) butter at room
temperature
30g (1oz) butter, melted, extra
50g (1¾oz/¼ cup) castor sugar
½ teaspoon vanilla extract
1 tablespoon castor sugar extra
2 organic free-range eggs
60ml (2fl oz/¼ cup) milk
160g (5½oz/1¼ cup) self-raising
flour
35g (1.2oz/¼ cup) custard powder
2 large apples, cored and finely
sliced (granny smith is best)
½ teaspoon cinnamon
12 paper cases

Apple Custard
AND CINNAMON MINI TEA CAKES

Makes 12 mini tea cakes

Combine all the custard ingredients in a saucepan stirring to combine. Boil until custard starts to thicken. Take off the heat and set aside to cool covering with plastic wrap directly onto the custard (to prevent a skin forming).

Preheat the oven to 180°C/160°C. Line a 12-hole muffin tin with paper cases.

Beat butter, sugar and vanilla together until light and fluffy. Then add eggs one at a time beating between additions. Add milk and then fold in the flour and custard powder.

Divide half the mixture between the 12-hole muffin tins. Top with the custard and then top with the remaining cake mixture to cover the custard. Divide the apple amongst each of the 12 cakes pressing in lightly.

Place in the oven and bake for 30 minutes. Once baked, remove from the oven, brush with extra melted hot butter and then lightly sprinkle with the extra sugar and cinnamon.

2 medium-sized oranges
3 teaspoons baking powder
9 organic free-range eggs
375g (13.2oz 1¾ cups) castor
sugar
1 vanilla bean halved and seeds
scraped out
300g (10oz/1⅓ cups) almond
meal
150g (5.2oz/1½ cups) desiccated
coconut
1½ teaspoon ground cinnamon

Candied Orange Zest
zest of 3 oranges
100g (3.5oz/½ cup) castor sugar
62.5ml (2 fl oz/¼ cup) water

Flourless Orange &
Almond Cake with Candied Orange Zest

Serves 24

Rinse oranges under hot water, then place in medium saucepan and cover with cold water. Bring to the boil and simmer uncovered for 40 minutes. Drain and allow to cool.

Preheat oven to 190°C/170°C. Grease 24-hole muffin tin and line base with paper.

Cut oranges in half, discard seeds. Blend or process oranges with baking powder until pulpy.

Beat eggs, sugar and vanilla bean seeds until pale and fluffy. Fold in almond meal, coconut, cinnamon and orange pulp.

Divide mixture evenly into muffin tins and bake for 25–30 minutes until golden and allow to cool in the tin.

Once cooled, remove from the tin and garnish with candied zest.

To make the candied orange zest: Remove rind from 3 oranges. Bring sugar and water together in a saucepan and simmer without boiling until sugar dissolves. Then add rind, simmer without stirring for 5 minutes.

Remove rind from syrup with tongs, spread on a wire rack to cool before using.

Tip Serve with your favourite side of cream—mascarpone is fantastic.

Angel Cake

160g (5½oz/1 cup) plain flour
250g (8oz/1 cup) castor sugar
¼ teaspoon salt
1¼ cups egg whites (from
approximately 10 organic free
range eggs) at room temperature
1½ teaspoon cream of tartar
2 teaspoon fresh lemon juice
zest of 1 lemon
1 fresh vanilla bean scraped
1 teaspoon vanilla essence
1½ cups Strawberry Cream (see
recipe on page 59)

Serves 10

Preheat the oven to 180°C (350°F). Using canola spray lightly spray and then line with greaseproof paper, a 25cm (10 in) round cake tin.

Sift together the flour, 1 cup sugar and salt. Do this 3 times and set aside.

Using a clean bowl, beat the egg whites at a medium-low speed until foamy, then add the cream of tartar. Increase the speed to medium-high and beat until whites are soft and foamy. Gradually beat in the remaining sugar until firm peaks have formed being careful not to overbeat. Then fold in the lemon juice, zest and vanilla.

Place the egg mixture into a large bowl and gently sift and fold in the flour mixture in 4 increments.

Scoop the batter into the cake tin and gently smooth the top. Bake for approximately 40 minutes until golden and cake springs back lightly to the touch. Allow to cool completely in the tin before turning out.

While the cake is cooking, make the strawberry cream (page 59 for recipe).

Allow the cake to cool completely, then using a large, serrated knife, cut the cake horizontally and spread the strawberry cream between the two halves. Serve with a spoonful of the strawberry cream on the side.

Tip To maximise the yield of the vanilla bean, cut lengthways, then with the blunt side of a knife scrape both sides of the bean, collecting the seeds.

175g (6oz) unsalted butter at
room temperature
200g (7oz/1 cup) castor sugar
zest of 3 lemons
4 organic free-range eggs separated
250g (8oz/1 cup) ricotta
125g (4oz/1 cup) self-raising flour
1 teaspoon baking powder

Lemon Ricotta Cake

Serves 12

Preheat the oven to 180°C (350°F).

Grease a 18cm (7 in) round cake tin.

Cream together the butter and sugar until pale and fluffy. Then add the zest, egg yolks and ricotta. Set aside.

In a separate bowl whip the egg whites to stiff peaks. Then gently fold into the ricotta mixture.

Fold in the flour and baking powder and then spoon mixture into the greased tin.

Bake for 35 minutes until risen, golden and firm to the touch. Cool in the tin before turning out.

Tip This cake is one of Joe's favourites and makes the most of his lemon tree. It is a recipe given to him by his grandmother and has been handed down through generations in his parent's hometown of Piedimonte Etneo in Sicily.

180g (6oz) butter at room
temperature
180g (6oz/1 cup) castor sugar
3 eggs
1 tablespoon vanilla essence
65ml (2fl oz/¼ cup) sunflower oil
100g (3½oz/1 cup) chopped
walnuts
250g (8oz/2 cups) self-raising
flour
1 teaspoon baking powder
2 tablespoons honey
65ml (2fl oz/¼ cup) sour cream
½ teaspoon ground cloves

Syrup
1 tablespoon honey
juice of 1 lemon

Icing
200g (7oz/1 cup) cream cheese
180g (6oz/1 cup) icing sugar,
sifted
juice of 1 lemon

Walnut

Babushka Cake

Makes approximately 8 slices

Preheat oven to 180°C (350°F) and grease and line a 20cm round cake tin with baking paper.

Beat together the butter and sugar until pale and fluffy.

Add the eggs, vanilla essence, oil and spice, then stir in the honey and sour cream.

Add the sifted flour and baking powder and whisk out any lumps.

Fold through the walnuts and pour batter into the cake tin.

Bake for 40 minutes at 180°C (350°F), and then reduce the heat to 160°C (310°F) for a further 20–30 minutes until a skewer comes out clean from the centre. Remove from the oven.

Mix together the honey and lemon juice, pour the mixture over the top of the cake and leave it to cool in the tin.

Meanwhile, beat together the cream cheese, lemon juice and icing sugar and spread over the cooled cake.

Tip If the cake is starting to darken too quickly in the oven, cover with a layer of baking paper and continue cooking.

200g (7oz/1 cup) unsalted butter at room temperature
150g (5oz/¾ cup) castor sugar
zest of 1 lemon
the seeds scraped from 1 vanilla bean
3 organic free-range eggs
160g (5½oz/1¼ cup) plain flour sifted
160g (5½oz/1¼ cup) self-raising flour sifted
1 teaspoon baking powder
300ml (10 fl oz) sour cream

Blueberry Filling
200g (7oz/1 cup) blueberries fresh or frozen
50g (1¾oz) brown sugar

Icing sugar to dust

Blueberry
AND SOUR CREAM CAKE

Preheat the oven to 180°C (350°F). Grease and line a 20cm loaf tin.

With an electric beater, cream together butter, sugar and lemon rind until pale and fluffy. Add the eggs one at a time beating after each addition along with the vanilla seeds.

Fold through the flours, baking powder and sour cream alternately until just combined.

Combine the filling ingredients. Pour half the cake batter into the prepared tin. Top with the blueberry filing. Add the remaining cake batter to cover. Bake for 1 hour and 10 minutes until top is golden and cake springs back lightly to the touch. Cool slightly. Then turn out onto a wire rack to cool completely.

Once completely cooled dust with icing sugar.

Tip Your favourite berry can be substituted for the blueberries. This moist cake will keep for up to 7 days if stored in an airtight container in the refrigerator but it won't last that long!

Crust
250g (8oz/1 cup) sweet biscuits (Scotch Finger, Milk Arrowroot or Granita)
100g (3½oz/½ cup) brown sugar
125g (4oz) butter, melted

Cheese Mixture
500g (1lb) cream cheese, softened
500g (1lb) mascarpone, softened
250g (8oz/1¼ cup) castor sugar
zest of 2 lemons
1 tablespoon vanilla essence
4 organic free-range eggs
raspberries to garnish

Mascarpone
AND RASPBERRY MINI CHEESECAKES

Makes 24 mini cheesecakes

Grease the bottom of a 24-hole muffin tin and line with baking paper.

Blend or process sweet biscuits until fine, then add sugar and blend again.

Pour in the melted butter until well combined.

Press the mixture into the bases of the muffin moulds and refrigerate for 30 minutes.

Preheat oven to 170°C (325°F).

To make the cheese filling: beat together cream cheese, mascarpone, sugar, zest and essence in a medium bowl with an electric mixer until smooth.

Beat in eggs, one at a time and be careful not to over beat.

Pour the mixture onto the biscuit bases while still in the moulds and top with desired raspberries.

Bake for 30–35 minutes.

Cool at room temperature then refrigerate.

Tip This recipe is great with mulberries when they are in season (early Spring through Summer).

375g (12¼oz/3 cups) plain flour,
sifted
130g (4oz/1 cup) unsweetened
cocoa, sifted
1½ teaspoon baking powder
½ teaspoon bicarbonate of soda
½ teaspoon salt
120g (4oz/½ cup) unsalted butter
at room temperature
395g (13½oz/1¾ cups, firmly
packed) brown sugar
2 teaspoon vanilla essence
4 organic free-range eggs
375ml (13 fl oz/1½ cups)
buttermilk at room temperature

Fudge Icing
375g dark chocolate finely chopped
435ml (15fl oz/1¾ cups) thickened
cream
125ml (4 fl oz/½ cup) sour cream
pinch of salt

Devils Chocolate Cake
WITH FUDGE ICING

Serves 10–12

Preheat the oven to 180°C (350°F). Grease and line two, 23cm (9 in) round cake tins.

Sift together the flour, cocoa, baking powder, soda and then add the salt.

In a separate bowl beat together the butter, sugar and vanilla until pale and fluffy. Then beat in the eggs one at a time, beating well between each addition.

Add the flour mixture in 3 batches alternating with the buttermilk.

Divide the mixture evenly between the 2 tins. Bake for 25–30 minutes until cooked and springs back lightly to the touch. Allow to cool in the tin for 15 minutes before turning out onto wire racks to completely cool.

Meanwhile make the icing: using a bain marie melt the chocolate and cream over a low heat until smooth. Allow to cool slightly before whisking in the sour cream and salt until just combined. Set aside icing to cool to room temperature stirring occasionally.

To assemble the cake, place one cake layer on a serving plate, then spread a third of the icing on top. Add the second layer of the cake onto the iced first layer pressing gently. Then spread the remaining icing over the entire cake.

Tip WARNING! Do Not Eat This Alone!

350g (12oz/2 cups) blanched almonds
200g (7oz/1 cup) castor sugar
250g (8oz/1 cup) dark chocolate, chopped
7 organic free-range eggs, separated
1 teaspoon vanilla essence
zest of 1 lemon
125ml (4fl oz/½ cup) melted butter, cooled to room temperature

Caprese Flourless
CHOCOLATE CAKE

Serves approximately 8

Preheat oven to 170°C (325°F) and grease a 10-inch round cake tin.

Combine almonds and ⅓ cup sugar in a processor and blend until almonds are finely ground.

Transfer the almond mixture to a medium bowl, do not clean the processor.

Add chocolate and ⅓ cup sugar and blend until chocolate is finely ground but not beginning to clump (about 30–40 seconds) then stir into the bowl of almond mix.

Using an electric mixer, beat egg yolks and remaining ⅓ cup sugar in a large bowl until mixture is thick and fluffy. The beat in vanilla and lemon zest.

Fold in the chocolate/almond mixture then melted butter.

Using a clean whisk, beat egg whites in a large bowl until stiff and fold gently into the chocolate batter in small additions, transfer to the prepared tin.

Bake cake until skewer comes out with no crumbs attached (about 40 minutes).

Cool cake completely and serve with dollop of mascarpone cheese.

400g (14oz/2 cups) castor sugar
250ml (8.5 fl oz/1 cup) vegetable oil
4 organic free-range eggs
320g (11oz/2½ cups) plain flour
2 teaspoons baking soda
2 teaspoons ground cinnamon
½ teaspoon ground ginger
1 teaspoon baking powder
½ teaspoon salt
500g (18oz/2 cups) cooked mashed
pumpkin
60g (3oz/½ cup) chopped pecans to
garnish

Cream Cheese Icing
40g (1½oz/¼ cup) butter
375g (13oz) cream cheese at room
temperature
250g (8oz/1¼ cup) icing sugar,
sifted
2 teaspoons vanilla extract

Spiced Pumpkin
TEA CAKES WITH CREAM CHEESE ICING

Serves 12

Preheat oven to 180°C (350°F). Grease 12-hole muffin tin.

Combine sugar, vegetable oil and eggs in a large bowl mixing well. Sift in the remaining dry ingredients and mix well. Stir in the mashed pumpkin.

Divide mixture amongst 12-hole muffin tin. Bake for 15-20 minutes until tops are golden and spring back lightly to the touch. Turn out onto a wire rack and cool completely.

Meanwhile combine all ingredients for cream cheese icing in a bowl and beat until smooth.

Once cakes have completely cooled, top with cream cheese icing and chopped pecans.

Tip For a nice, nutty texture, use butternut pumpkin, as Jap pumpkins can be a little stringy.

360g (11¾oz/2¾ cups) self-
raising flour
90g (3oz/⅓ cup) butter cold and
roughly chopped
200g (7oz/1 cup) castor sugar
315ml (10 fl oz/1¼ cups)
buttermilk
1 teaspoon vanilla essence

1 organic free-range egg lightly
beaten
25g (0.8oz/⅓ cup) desiccated
coconut
200g (7oz/1 cup) ricotta
150g (5oz) fresh or frozen
raspberries
2 tablespoons shredded coconut

Raspberry
AND RICOTTA MUFFIN

Makes 12 muffins

Preheat the oven to 180°C/160°C. Grease a 12-hole muffin tin.

Sift flour into a medium bowl. Rub in butter with fingertips. Add sugar, buttermilk, egg, vanilla essence and desiccated coconut stirring to combine with no lumps. Then add ricotta and raspberries stirring until just combined.

Divide mixture evenly into the 12-hole muffin tin. Top with shredded coconut.

Bake for 20 minutes until golden and the muffins are firm to the touch.

Tip Fresh Italian ricotta is preferable. You can substitute frozen berries when fresh raspberries aren't in season, just make sure if you are using frozen berries to use them straight from the freezer otherwise they will bleed into the mixture.

125g (4½oz/1 cup) chopped dates
125ml (4 fl oz/½ cup) warm water
1 teaspoon vanilla essence
360g (11¾oz/2¾ cups) self-raising flour
55g (1½oz/⅓ cup) plain flour
1 teaspoon ground cinnamon, plus ½ teaspoon extra
½ teaspoon bicarbonate of soda
100g (3½oz/½ cup, firmly packed) brown sugar
1 cup mashed banana
2 organic free-range eggs slightly beaten
185ml (6 fl oz/¾ cup) buttermilk
85ml (2½oz/⅓ cup) vegetable oil

Glaze
1 tablespoon unsalted butter
75ml maple syrup
1 tablespoon brown sugar

Date and Banana Muffin
WITH MAPLE SYRUP GLAZE

Makes 12 muffins

Preheat the oven to 200°C/180°C. Grease a 12-hole muffin tin.

To make the muffins: combine dates and water in a small saucepan and bring to the boil and reduce slightly. Set aside to cool.

Sift flours, cinnamon and baking soda into a large bowl.

In a separate bowl combine banana, eggs, buttermilk, oil and brown sugar. Add to the flour mixture along with the cooled date mixture and fold through until combined. Divide evenly amongst 12-hole muffin tin.

Bake for 20 minutes until golden and firm to the touch.

While muffins are baking, add the ingredients for the glaze in a small saucepan and heat to combine.

Once the muffins are cooked and have started to cool, brush with the warm maple glaze.

Tip You can use our VR Cream Cheese icing (see page 87) instead of the Maple Syrup Glaze, which works nicely with this recipe too.

2 organic free-range eggs
125ml (4 fl oz/½ cup) milk
125ml (4 fl oz/½ cup) vegetable oil
*320g (11oz/2½ cups) self-raising
flour, sifted*
1 tablespoon smoked paprika
1 tablespoon sea salt
2 teaspoon white pepper
60g (3oz/¾ cup) grated Parmesan
*250g (8oz/1 cup) roasted capsicum,
chopped*
½ bunch fresh thyme, chopped
*60g (3oz/¼ cup) seeded black olives,
chopped*
mascarpone cheese to serve

Olive Tapenade
1 clove of garlic
1 anchovy fillet
65ml (3fl oz/¼ cup) olive oil
*150g (5½oz) kalamata olives,
pitted*
½ bunch fresh basil
juice of 1 lemon

Roast Capsicum
AND PAPRIKA MUFFINS WITH OLIVE TAPENADE AND MASCARPONE CHEESE

Makes 24 muffins

Preheat oven to 180°C (350°F) and grease a 24-hole muffin tin.

To make the muffins: Beat eggs, milk and oil together on a large bowl until well combined.

Slowly add the flour and seasoning and whisk out any lumps.

Fold through the cheese, capsicum, thyme and chopped olives.

Divide the mixture evenly into the muffin tins and bake for 15–20 minutes.

Remove from the oven and cool for 10 minutes then cut off the tops.

Make the olive tapenade: Process all ingredients except the oil until a paste has formed.

Spread the tapenade on the bottom half and sandwich the two halves together.

Slowly add in oil and lemon juice.

Serve with a dollop of mascarpone cheese.

9 Roma or egg tomatoes
salt and pepper for seasoning
250ml (8fl oz/1 cup) vegetable oil
100g (3½oz/½ cup) castor sugar
200g (7oz) Persian feta
4 large organic free-range eggs
375g (12¼oz/3 cups) plain flour,
sifted
4 cups shredded zucchini
(courgette) (wring out moisture
by rolling them in a tea towel and
squeezing)
2 teaspoons baking soda
½ teaspoon baking powder
1 teaspoon ground white pepper
100g (3½oz/½ cup) grated
parmesan
1 bunch fresh thyme, chopped

Roast Tomato, Zucchini,
PARMESAN AND FETA MUFFIN

Makes 18 muffins

Sprinkled quartered roma tomatoes with salt and pepper and place on a wire rack in a preheated oven at 150°C (300°F) for approximately 30 minutes until roasted.

Once the tomatoes have reduced in size, remove from the oven and allow to cool.

Mix together the oil, sugar and eggs.

Add the shredded zucchini, flour, baking soda, baking powder and salt and pepper until well combined.

Fold through the parmesan and thyme.

Lightly grease 18-hole muffin tin and fill each half way to the top.

Lay two wedges of tomato on the top and garnish with a couple of cubes of the feta.

Bake for 20–25 minutes at 170°C (325°F).

zest of 2 lemons
125ml (4fl oz/½ cup) lemon juice
7 eggs
300ml (4fl oz) thickened cream
150g (5oz/¾ cup) castor sugar
1 vanilla bean, scraped of seeds
7 drops of edible essential lavender oil
extra raw sugar for toffee crust

Individual Lavender
CRÈME BRULEE IN A TEA CUP

Makes approximately 12 espresso cups, tea cups will vary in size effecting quantities.

In a medium bowl, whisk all ingredients together until well combined.

Pour into small teacups (or espresso cups work well if your tea cups are delicate).

Place the cups on a large baking tray and pour in hot water to about half way up the cup.

Cover the cups and cook in the oven for approximately 30 minutes at 170°C (325°F).

Allow to cool at room temperature before refrigerating.

Sprinkle the brulee with a little extra raw sugar and with a flame burner, wave over the top until the sugar melts and turns brown. Allow this to set for a lovely crispy, sweet toffee.

Tip Make sure you check with your shop assistant that your essential oil is edible and able to be ingested.

Pastry

320g (11oz/2½ cups) plain flour sifted
50g (1½oz/⅓ cup) icing sugar
30g (1oz/¼ cup) corn flour
½ teaspoon salt
250g (8oz/1 cup) unsalted butter at room temperature

Filling

4 organic free-range eggs lightly beaten
265g (9oz/1¼ cup) castor sugar
3 tablespoons plain flour sifted
zest of 2 lemons
165ml (5½ fl oz/⅔ cup) lemon juice
85ml (2¾fl oz/⅓ cup) milk
¼ teaspoon salt
icing sugar to dust

Deluxe Lemon Slice

Makes 24–30 depending on size of the squares.

Preheat the oven to 170°C (325°F). Grease and line 30cm x 20cm (12 x 8in) rectangular baking dish.

In a food processor, pulse all dry ingredients until well combined, add the butter and pulse until the mixture comes together and resembles coarse meal.

Scatter the meal over the base of the prepared tin and press firmly into an even layer with slightly raised sides to hold in the filling.

Refrigerate for 20 minutes and then bake for 20 minutes. Remove from oven and cool slightly.

Reduce oven to 150°C (300°F).

To make the filling: in a medium bowl whisk together eggs, sugar and flour. Then stir in juice, zest, milk and salt and mix until combined. Pour filling over warm crust and bake for a further 15–20 minutes. Cool completely before lifting out of tray and serving. Cut into squares and dust with icing sugar.

Tip Use a hot knife when slicing to avoid the mixture sticking to the knife and cracking the pastry.

600g (1¼ lb/3½ cups) dark chocolate chopped
6 tablespoons water
300g (10oz/1⅓ cups) unsalted butter
1 tablespoon vanilla essence
300g (10oz/1½ cups) castor sugar
6 organic free-range eggs lightly beaten
160g (5½oz/1¼ cup) plain flour, sifted
450g (13½oz/2½ cups) white chocolate roughly chopped
500g (1lb/3½ cups) hazelnuts roughly chopped

Decadent Choc-Hazelnut

BROWNIES

Makes approximately 30 squares

Preheat the oven to 180°C (350°F). Grease and line a 30 x 40cm (12 x 16 in) tin.

Combine chocolate, water, butter and vanilla essence over a bain marie until smooth. Then add the sugar and stir through until dissolved. Remove from the heat.

Whisk in the lightly beaten eggs, flour and fold until just combined.

Then gently stir through the white chocolate and nuts being careful not to over mix.

Pour into the prepared tin, smoothing the top of the mixture and bake for 15–20 minutes. Allow to cool slightly in the tin before turning out to cool on a wire rack.

Cut into squares and serve.

Tip As there is very little flour in this recipe, be careful not to over cook the brownies. It will set when cooled.

Tarts

Sweet Short Crust Pastry

*400g (13oz/3 cups) plain flour
sifted
100g (3½oz/½ cup) castor sugar
½ vanilla bean scraped
zest of 1 lemon
180g (6oz/¾ cup) unsalted, cold,
diced butter
3 organic free-range egg yolks
60–80ml (2–2¾fl oz) cold soda
water*

Filling

*3 organic free-range eggs
6 organic free-range yolks
300g (10oz/1½cups) castor sugar
zest and juice of 4 lemons
zest and juice of 3 limes
350ml (11 fl oz/1⅓ cups) double
cream*

Mini Lemon
AND LIME TART

Makes 18 tarts

To make the filling: whisk in the egg yolks and eggs with the sugar, juice and zest until sugar is dissolved. Add the cream to the egg mixture and lightly whisk, being careful not to over whisk. Rest custard for half an hour in the refrigerator and skim excess foam before pouring into the tart cases.

To make the pastry: Place the flour, sugar, vanilla, zest and butter in a food processor and process until mixture resembles fine bread crumbs.

Add the egg yolks and the soda water slowly and process until mixture comes together to form a soft biscuit-like dough. Make sure to only use as much soda water as you need. You may not need it all.

Turn the dough onto a lightly floured surface and knead until just smooth. Shape into a round disk, cover with plastic wrap and refrigerate for 30 minutes.

Preheat oven to 180°C (350°F) and grease 18, 7cm (3 in) (base measurement) fluted tart tins. Divide pastry into 18 equal pieces and roll out to a 3mm (¹/₈ in) thickness.

Line tart tins with the pastry making sure to press into the corners, place on baking trays and refrigerate for 15 minutes. Blind bake for 5–6 minutes until set. Remove the baking paper and baking weights and bake for a further 3–5 minutes until golden.

Reduce oven to 150°C (300°F). Pour the custard into the pastry cases bake for a further 10–15 minutes or until just set. Remove from the oven and set aside for 15 minutes to cool.

Tip Substitute lime for fresh passionfruit pulp and proceed as per the instructions above.

Pastry

60g (2oz/¼ cup) unsalted butter
at room temperature
60g (2oz/⅓ cup) castor sugar
2 organic free-range eggs
60g (3oz) dark chocolate melted
350g (11¾oz/2¾ cups) plain flour
1 tablespoon cocoa powder
1 pinch salt

Filling

400g (14oz/2⅓ cups) dark
chocolate
700ml (24 fl oz/2⅓ cups)
thickened cream
3 organic free-range eggs
200g (7oz/1 cup) castor sugar
1 tablespoon vanilla essence

Chocolate Fudge Tart

Serves 12–16

Make the pastry: cream together butter and sugar. Once pale and fluffy add the eggs one at a time then the melted chocolate. Sift in cocoa, plain flour and salt. Place dough on a lightly floured surface and knead until just coming together. Press flat into a round shape, cover with plastic wrap and rest for 30 minutes in the refrigerator.

Grease 24cm round loose-based flan tin. Once rested, remove plastic wrap and place pastry dough between 2 pieces of greaseproof paper that have been pre cut to fit the flan tin. Roll pastry to approximately 5mm (¼ in) thick. Cover and refrigerate for 30 minutes.

Preheat oven to 180°C (350°F). Place flan tin on a tray, cover pastry case with baking paper and fill with bakers beans and blind bake for 15 minutes. Remove paper and beans and bake uncovered for a further 10 minutes. Cool pastry shell.

Make the filling: using a bain marie melt chocolate and cream together stirring until smooth. In a separate bowl, whisk together eggs, sugar and vanilla essence. Then combine with the chocolate cream.

Pour into cooled pastry shell and bake in oven at 170°C/150°C (325°F/300°F) for 15–20 minutes or until set and slightly wobbly in the centre.

Tip Bakers beans are dried beans placed on the pastry shell to prevent the centre from rising or bubbling up. Pricking with a fork may also help prevent air pockets expanding in the heat. Placing one saucepan on top of another filled with simmering water can make a bain marie. Do not allow any water into the melting chocolate.

125g (4½oz) dark chocolate
1 teaspoon hazelnut paste
3 organic free-range eggs,
separated
200g (7oz/1 cup) castor sugar
15ml (1 tablespoon) Amaretto
liqueur
250ml (8fl oz) thickened cream
approximately 50 fresh raspberries
approximately 50 mini chocolate
cups (see tips)
Chantilly cream for topping (see
page 58)

Dark Chocolate Cups

WITH CHOCOLATE MOUSSE
AND FRESH RASPBERRIES

Makes 50 cups

Melt chocolate and hazelnut paste together over a Bain Marie (don't mix or stir).

In a separate bowl, whisk egg whites and half the sugar until stiff peaks form.

In another bowl, whisk egg yolks and remaining sugar until pale then add the Amaretto.

In another bowl, whip the cream until airy and light, then fold the chocolate through gently as to not deflate the cream.

Add the egg yolk mix to the chocolate mixture then gently fold through the egg white mix.

Set the mousse in the refrigerator for approximately 30 minutes then scrape into a piping bag.

Arrange the chocolate cup moulds on a tray and pipe the mousse into them to ¾ full.

Top with a drop of Chantilly Cream (see page 58) and garnish with a fresh raspberry on top.

Tip Mini chocolate cup moulds and hazlenut paste can be bought at quality gourmet delis, confectionary stores and leading department stores.

Cream Patisserie

300ml (10.2 fl oz) milk
300ml (10.2 fl oz) pouring cream
1 vanilla bean, deseeded
4 organic free-range egg yolks
125g (4¾oz/⅔cup) castor sugar
1 tablespoon corn flour

Sweet Short Crust Pastry

400g (14oz/2½ cups) plain flour,
sifted
100g (3½oz/½ cup) castor sugar
½ vanilla bean scraped
zest of 1 lemon
180g (6oz/¾ cup) unsalted cold
diced butter
3 organic free-range egg yolks
60–80ml (2–2¾fl oz) cold soda
water

500g (17½oz) or approximately
18 medium strawberries
icing sugar to dust

Strawberry Tartlets

WITH CREAM PATISSERIE

Makes approximately 18 mini tartlets

Make the cream patisserie: Over a low to medium heat, warm the milk, cream and vanilla bean together.

In a separate bowl, beat egg yolks with sugar and corn flour until thick. Pour the egg mix into the warm milk/cream mix and stir continuously over moderate heat until the liquid has thickened.

Allow to cool at room temperature, meanwhile bake your pastry in your desired tart shell moulds and allow to cool.

Preheat oven to 180°C (350°F) and grease 18, 7cm (3 in) (base measurement) fluted tart tins.

To make the pastry: Place the flour, sugar, vanilla, zest and butter in a food processor and process until mixture resembles fine bread crumbs. Add the egg yolks and the soda water slowly and process until mixture comes together to form a soft biscuit-like dough. Make sure to only use as much soda water as you need. You may not need it all.

Turn the dough onto a lightly floured surface and knead until just smooth. Shape into a round disk, cover with plastic wrap and refrigerate for 30 minutes.

Divide pastry into 18 equal pieces and roll out to a 3mm (¹/₈ in) thickness. Line to tart tins with the pastry making sure to press into the corners. Place tart tins on baking trays and refrigerate for 15 minutes.

Blind bake for 5–6 minutes for until set. Remove the baking paper and baking weights and bake for a further 3–5 minutes until golden.

Spoon the cream into tart shells, top with strawberries and dust patisserie with icing sugar.

Sweet Short Crust Pastry

*400g (14oz/2½ cups) plain flour
sifted*
100g (3½oz/½ cup) castor sugar
½ vanilla bean scraped
zest of 1 lemon
*180g (6oz/¾ cup) unsalted, cold,
diced butter*
3 organic free-range egg yolks
*60-80ml (2-2¾fl oz) cold soda
water*

Filling

300ml (10fl oz) thickened cream
*300g (10oz/1⅓ cups) white
chocolate*
1 vanilla bean scraped
6 organic free-range egg yolks

Icing sugar for dusting
9 figs quartered

Individual Tart of Fig
AND VANILLA BEAN WITH WHITE CHOCOLATE

Makes 18 tartlets

To make the filling: in a heatproof bowl over a bain marie, combine the cream, chocolate and vanilla and heat until smooth. Whisk in egg yolks individually, being careful not to overheat, as eggs will scramble. Once custard coats the back of a wooden spoon, set aside to cool. Place a sheet of grease proof paper directly over the custard to prevent a skin forming.

Make the pastry: Place the flour, sugar, vanilla, zest and butter in a food processor until mixture resembles fine breadcrumbs. Add egg yolks and the soda water slowly until mixture comes together. Use as much soda water as you need—you may not need it all.

Turn the dough onto a lightly-floured surface and knead until just smooth. Shape into a round disk, cover with plastic wrap and refrigerate for 30 minutes.

Preheat oven to 180°C (350°F) and grease 18 x 7cm (3 in) (base measurement) fluted tart tins. Divide pastry into 18 equal pieces and roll out to a 3mm (⅛ in) thickness. Line tart tins with the pastry making sure to press into the corners. Place tart tins on baking trays and refrigerate for 15 minutes.

Blind bake for 5–6 minutes for until set. Remove the baking paper and baking weights and bake for a further 3–5 minutes until golden.

Reduce oven to 150°C (300°F). Evenly distribute the quartered figs into the pastry cases. Pour over the custard to cover and bake for a further 10–15 minutes or until just set. Remove from the oven and set aside for 15 minutes to cool. Place the tarts in the refrigerator to chill.

Preheat a grill on high, dust tartlets with icing sugar and cook for 1–2 minutes or until top caramelises. Serve with cream or mascarpone.

Sweet Short Crust Pastry

400g (14oz/2½ cups) plain flour sifted
100g (3½oz/½ cup) castor sugar
½ vanilla bean scraped
zest of 1 lemon
180g (6oz/¾ cup) unsalted, cold, diced butter
3 organic free-range egg yolks
60-80ml (2-2¾fl oz) cold soda water

Panacotta

500ml thickened cream
250ml (8fl oz/1 cup) whole milk
150g (5oz/¾ cup) castor sugar
2 vanilla bean pods with seeds removed
20ml (0.7 fl oz) rose water
2 gelatin sheets
rose petals and icing sugar for dusting

Chilled Rose

PANACOTTA TART WITH ROSE PETALS

Makes 18 mini tarts

Make the pastry: Place the flour, sugar, vanilla, zest and butter in a food processor until mixture resembles fine breadcrumbs. Add egg yolks and the soda water slowly until mixture comes together. Use as much soda water as you need—you may not need it all.

Turn the dough onto a lightly floured surface and knead until just smooth. Shape into a round disk, cover with plastic wrap and refrigerate for 30 minutes.

Preheat oven to 180°C (350°F) and grease 18, 7cm (3 in) (base measurement) fluted tart tins. Divide pastry into 18 equal pieces and roll out to a 3mm (¹/₈ in) thickness.

Line tart tins with the pastry making sure to press into the corners. Place tart tins on baking trays and refrigerate for 15 minutes.

Blind bake for 5–6 minutes until set. Remove the baking paper and baking weights and bake for a further 3–5 minutes until golden.

To make the panacotta: in a medium saucepan, combine the cream, milk, sugar, vanilla and rose water. Bring to a gentle simmer and allow to stand for 10 minutes. Then add gelatin and stir until dissolved.

Allow to stand for another 5 minutes and then strain into a shallow dish and set in the refrigerator for approximately 45–60 minutes.

Spoon the panacotta mix into tart shells and garnish with rose petals and dusted icing sugar, serve immediately.

Tip If you are pushed for time then buy ready made sweet tart shells from gourmet delis and kitchenware stores.

1 leek, finely sliced
60g (2oz) butter
120g (3.8oz) pancetta, sliced
½ bunch fresh thyme, chopped
1 teaspoon sea salt
1 teaspoon black pepper
3 organic free-range eggs
300ml (10.2fl oz) pouring cream

Tart Shells
200g (7oz/1 cup) cold, diced butter
400g (14oz/2½ cups) plain flour
2 teaspoons sea salt
80-100ml (2¾-3½fl oz) cold soda
water
3 organic free-range egg yolks

Pancetta, Leek
AND THYME TARTLETS

Makes 18 tartlets

Make the filling: In a fry pan, gently sauté leeks in butter, then add pancetta, thyme and seasoning.

Remove from heat and cool completely.

In a separate bowl, whisk eggs and cream and combine with leek mixture.

Preheat oven to 180°C (350°F).

Make the pastry: In a large bowl, rub together butter, flour and salt until resembling bread crumbs.

Add soda water and egg yolks working through until a soft dough has formed.

Grease an 18-hole tart tray and roll out dough to approximately 5mm (¼ in) thick on a floured bench.

Using a round cookie cutter or egg ring, cut out rounds of pastry and press into the tart moulds and bake for approximately 10–15 minutes.

Divide mixture into tart shells and bake until golden brown.

Tip approximately 18 tartlets depending on mould size.

3 brown onions, sliced
3 tablespoons olive oil
100ml (3½fl oz) balsamic vinegar
100g (3½oz/½ cup) brown sugar
250g (8oz/1 cup) goats cheese
½ bunch fresh thyme
300ml (10fl oz) cream
3 organic free-range eggs
pepper for seasoning

Tart Shells
200g (7oz/1 cup) cold, diced butter
400g (13oz/3 cups) plain flour
2 teaspoon sea salt
80-100ml (2¾-3½fl oz) cold soda water
3 organic free-range egg yolks

Caramelised Balsamic Onion
AND GOATS CHEESE TARTS

Makes 18 tartlets

Preheat oven to 180°C (350°F).

Make the pastry: In a large bowl, rub together butter, flour and salt until resembling bread crumbs.

Add soda water and egg yolks working through until a soft dough has formed.

Grease an 18-hole tart tray and roll out dough on a floured bench to approximately 5mm (¼ in) thick.

Using a round cookie cutter or egg ring, cut out rounds of pastry and press into the tart moulds and bake for approximately 10–15 minutes.

Make the filling: in a fry pan, sauté onions in oil over a low heat until reduced.

Mix through balsamic vinegar and sugar and cook till resembling a jam consistency.

When the jam has cooled, divide the mixture into the tart shells and place a cube or teaspoon of goats cheese in the centre.

Whisk together the cream and eggs and pour into the tart shells and sprinkle with pepper and thyme to season.

Bake until mixture is golden brown, approximately 10-12 minutes in a medium oven.

Sweet Short Crust Pastry

400g (13oz/3 cups) plain flour sifted
100g (3½oz/½ cup) castor sugar
½ vanilla bean scraped
zest of 1 lemon
180g (6oz/¾ cup) unsalted, cold, diced butter
3 organic free-range egg yolks
60-80ml (2-2¾fl oz) cold soda water

Frangipane Mix

200g (6½oz) unsalted butter at room temperature
200g (7oz/1 cup) castor sugar
3 organic free-range eggs
40g (1½oz/⅓ cup) plain flour, sifted
200g (7oz/2 cups) almond meal
250g (8oz/1 cup) fresh raspberries
250g (8oz/1 cup) fresh blueberries
250g (8oz/1 cup) fresh strawberries cut in halves
65g (2oz/¼ cup) strawberry jam, plus 2 tablespoons for syrup (see Conserves section)

Rustic Flan

WITH SEASONAL BERRIES AND ALMOND FRANGIPANE

Makes 18 flans

Make the pastry: Place the flour, sugar, vanilla, zest and butter in a food processor until mixture resembles fine breadcrumbs. Add egg yolks and the soda water slowly until mixture comes together. Use as much soda water as you need—you may not need it all.

Turn the dough onto a lightly floured surface and knead until just smooth. Shape into a round disk, cover with plastic wrap and refrigerate for 30 minutes.

Preheat oven to 180°C (350°F) and grease 18 x 7cm (3 in) (base measurement) fluted tart tins. Divide pastry into 18 equal pieces and roll out to a 3mm (⅛ in) thickness. Line tart tins with the pastry, making sure to press into the corners.

Place tart tins on baking trays and refrigerate for 15 minutes. Blind bake for 5–6 minutes for until set. Remove the baking paper and baking weights and bake for a further 3–5 minutes until golden.

To make frangipane mix: beat together butter and sugar until pale and fluffy, then add eggs slowly, one at a time. When combined, add flour and almond meal, stir through. Then spread the strawberry jam on the base of the tart. Add the frangipane mix to the tart shells and top with the mixed berries.

Bake for 15–20 minutes at 170°C (325°F) until golden brown and cooked in the centre. While tarts are cooking, combine the 2 tablespoons of jam with 2 tablespoons of water and stir over a low heat, to form a syrup.

Remove the tarts from the oven an brush the tops with syrup. Allow tarts to cool before serving with a dollop of mascarpone.

Biscuits

260g (8oz/1¼ cup) unsalted cold butter diced
125g (4oz/½ cup) castor sugar
250g (8oz/2 cups) plain flour sifted
2–3 drops of lavender oil
125g (4oz/1 cup) rice flour sifted

Topping
40g (1½oz/¼ cup) castor sugar
2 dried lavender flowers

Lavender Shortbreads

Makes 24 shortbreads (depending on biscuit shape)

Preheat the oven to 160°C (310°F). Grease and line 2 baking trays.

To make the shortbread: cream together butter, sugar and lavender oil until light and fluffy.

Work in the mixed flours. Turn onto a lightly floured surface and roll dough in between 2 sheets of baking paper approximately 1 cm thick.

Cut into your favourite shape; prick all over with a fork. Refrigerate for 15 minutes before baking for 10–12 minutes until golden.

While biscuits are baking, process sugar and lavender flowers until very fine.

Once the hot biscuits are removed from the oven, sprinkle with the sugar and lavender flower mixture. Then allow to completely cool before serving.

Tip Lavender flowers and oil can be purchased at health food stores. Check with store assistants before purchasing oil for cooking purposes.

250g (8oz/1¼ cup) unsalted butter
55g (1½oz/⅓ cup) icing sugar
1 teaspoon vanilla essence
200g (6¾oz/1½ cup) self-raising flour sifted
70g (2¼oz/½ cup) custard powder

Filling

60g (3oz) unsalted butter
60g (3oz/½ cup) icing sugar
2 tablespoons fresh passion fruit pulp
2–3 drops yellow food colouring

Melting Moments
WITH PASSIONFRUIT FILLING

Makes 23 biscuits

Preheat the oven to 170°C (325°F). Grease and line 2 baking trays.

Beat together butter, sugar and vanilla until light and fluffy.

Stir in the remaining sifted dry ingredients in 2 batches.

Roll even teaspoons of the mixture into balls and place onto the prepared trays. Using a floured fork press down lightly onto the balls.

Refrigerate for 15 minutes and then bake for 10 minutes or until biscuits are firm. Allow to cool completely.

While biscuits are cooling make the filling—beat together all the ingredients until well combined.

Once biscuits are completely cool, spread one half of the biscuit with the filling and sandwich together with another biscuit. Repeat for the remainder of the biscuits.

120g (4oz/½ cup) butter at room temperature
300g (10oz/1½ cups) castor sugar
1 organic free-range egg
juice and zest of 3 lemons
465g (16½oz/3¾ cups) plain flour
½ teaspoon baking soda
pinch of salt

Lemon Icing
55g (2oz/¼ cup) unsalted butter at room temperature
1 teaspoon grated lemon zest
125ml (4fl oz/½ cup) lemon juice
515g (1lb/4 cups) icing sugar mixture

Candied Lemon Zest
rind of 3 lemons
100g (3½oz/½ cup) castor sugar
65ml (2fl oz/¼ cup) water

High Tea Lemon Cookies
WITH CANDIED LEMON

Serves

Preheat the oven to 180°C (350°F).

With an electric beater, combine butter and sugar until pale and fluffy. Beat in the egg, lemon juice and zest.

In a separate bowl sift together flour and baking soda and then add the salt. Gradually fold the flour mixture to the butter mixture until a dough forms. Wrap the mixture in plastic wrap and refrigerate for 1 hour.

After mixture has rested, roll heaped tablespoons of the dough into round balls. Place balls 2 inches apart on lined baking trays.

Bake for 12–15 minutes until golden. Place on wire racks to cool completely.

While cookies are cooling, make the lemon icing. In a separate bowl mix together all the ingredients for the lemon icing until smooth.

Once cookies have completely cooled top with the lemon icing and garnish with the candied lemon zest.

Make the lemon zest using a string zest: remove rind from 3 lemons. Bring sugar and water together in a saucepan and simmer without boiling until sugar dissolves. Then add rind, simmer without stirring for 5 minutes.

Remove rind from syrup with metal tongs, spread on a wire rack to cool before using.

Tip When making the candied lemon zest, try to use organic lemons, as they usually won't have the wax coating that supermarket ones have.

250g (8oz/1¼ cup) unsalted butter
at room temperature
1 teaspoon vanilla essence
100g (3½oz/½ cup) castor sugar
300g (10oz/2⅓ cups) plain flour
sifted
2 teaspoons sea salt
200g (7oz/1 cup) hazelnuts
coarsely ground
100g (3½oz) dark chocolate melted

Chocolate Dipped
HAZELNUT SHORTBREAD ROUNDS

Makes 24 biscuits

Preheat the oven to 200°C (400°F). Grease and line 2 baking trays.

Cream together butter, vanilla and sugar until light and fluffy.

Fold in the flour, salt and hazelnuts. Turn onto a lightly floured surface and roll dough in between 2 sheets of baking paper approximately 1 cm thick.

Cut into your favourite shape. Refrigerate for 15 minutes before baking for 10–15 minutes until golden. Allow to completely cool.

Once biscuits are cool, dip half of the biscuit into the melted chocolate and place on greaseproof paper to set. Repeat with remaining biscuits.

Tip For a romantic treat use a small heart shaped cutter and then follow the instructions as above.

300g (10oz, 3 cups) almond meal
3 organic free-range egg whites
lightly beaten
200g (7oz, 1 cup) castor sugar
1 cup flaked almonds
3 drops almond essence
3 teaspoons vanilla Galliano

Italian

ALMOND HORSE SHOES

Makes 24 biscuits

Preheat the oven to 190°C/170°C.

Combine the almond meal, egg whites, sugar, vanilla essence and Galliano in a medium bowl until just combined.

Roll heaped tablespoons of the mixture into a log then roll over the flaked almonds to coat.

Shape the rolls into horseshoes and place on baking paper on oven trays.

Bake for approximately 15–18 minutes.

Tip With much convincing and begging, Joe's wife Chrystalla kindly let us use this recipe of hers. 'She makes them with love for me and I hope you love them too' says Joe.

400g (13oz/3cups) plain flour sifted
1 teaspoon baking powder
3 organic free range eggs
200g (7oz/1 cup) castor sugar
150g blanched almonds
150g pistachios
zest and juice of 2 lemons
1 tablespoon vanilla essence
1 tablespoon rosewater

Pistachio, Lemon
AND ALMOND BISCOTTI

Makes 40 thin biscotti

Preheat the oven to 170°C (325°F). Grease and line a 20cm (8 in) loaf tin.

Combine flour and baking powder in a bowl.

In a separate bowl, whisk together the eggs, sugar, zest, juice, vanilla and rosewater.

Slowly whisk in the flour mixture into the egg mixture until combined making sure to whisk out the lumps.

Fold in the pistachios and almonds to the mixture and then pour the batter into the prepared loaf tin.

Bake for 45 minutes, and then turn down the oven to 140°C (275°F) and bake for a further 20 minutes until a skewer inserted into the centre comes out clean. Allow to cool for 10 minutes in the tin, turn out onto a wire rack and cool completely.

Place in the refrigerator for 1 hour, then thinly slice the loaf approximately 3mm–5mm ($1/8$–¼ in). Place biscotti on a lined baking tray and bake for a further 10–15 minutes at 100°C (225°F) or until crispy.

Serve with your favourite coffee or tea.

Tip We like to serve these with our Chocolate Mousse or simply with a good coffee.

6 organic free-range egg whites
200g (7oz, 1 cup) castor sugar
6 teaspoon Dutch cocoa
2 teaspoon hot water
25g (⅓ cup) desiccated coconut
2 teaspoon vanilla essence

Chocolate Ganache
200g (7oz/1 cup) dark cooking
chocolate
½ cup thickened cream
1 tablespoon confectioners sugar

Coconut and Dutch Chocolate

MACAROONS WITH CHOCOLATE FUDGE CENTRE

Makes 20 macaroons

Preheat the oven to 150°C (300°F). Grease and line a baking tray with grease proof paper.

Whip the egg whites until very stiff gradually adding the sugar.

In a separate small bowl dissolve the cocoa in a little hot water to form a thin paste.

Gradually add the cocoa mixture to the whipped egg whites and lastly add the coconut.

Place teaspoonfuls on the prepared trays and bake for 45 minutes then allow the macaroons to cool in the oven with the door ajar until completely cooled.

Meanwhile make the ganache—using a bain marie stir together the chocolate, confectioners sugar and thickened cream until smooth. Take off the heat and allow to cool, stirring occasionally until cool enough to spread and is of an icing consistency.

Spread the ganache onto a macaroon and sandwich together with another macaroon.

Tip Confectioners sugar is like icing sugar with corn flour. You can find it in the cake-making aisle at most major supermarkets—Joe

Strawberry Jam

¼ quantity of organic strawberry jam (see Conserves, page 66).

250g (8oz/1¼ cup) unsalted butter, softened
230g (8oz/1 cup) castor sugar
2 organic free-range eggs
½ teaspoon vanilla essence
250g (8oz/2 cups) plain flour, sifted
250g (8oz/2 cups) self-raising flour, sifted
200g (7oz/1 cup) white chocolate for garnish

Simple Jam Heart
BISCUITS

Makes approximately 24 biscuits, depending on cookie cutter size.

To make the jam: in a heavy based saucepan add all ingredients and stir over low heat until sugar is dissolved.

Increase heat to high and bring mixture to the boil. Then turn down and cook for 20–30 minutes stirring often. Allow to cool.

Preheat oven to 160°C (310°F) and line a large baking try with grease proof paper.

To make the biscuits: using electric beaters, cream together the butter and sugar until pale and fluffy. Add eggs and vanilla until well combined. Fold the flours through until a soft dough forms.

Turn the dough out onto a sheet of baking paper and place another on top. Roll the dough to approximately 5mm (¼ in) thick.

Using a large heart shaped cookie cutter, cut out your biscuits.

Place half on the baking tray and with the other half, use a small heart shaped cutter to cut out the center of the cookies forming a framed window. Place these on your baking tray.

Bake for 10–15 minutes or until lightly golden. Remove from the oven and cool completely on a wire rack.

Once cooled, spread the base heart cookie with the jam and sandwich with the heart frame cookie to show a window of jam in the centre.

To garnish, melt the chocolate in a bain marie and pour into a piping bag. Drizzle the biscuits with the chocolate and set in the refrigerator for 10 minutes before serving.

1 cup sweetened condensed milk
2 teaspoons honey
30g (1oz) unsalted butter
1 tablespoon castor sugar
1 tablespoon plain flour
1 cup sultanas
2 cups corn flakes
1 cup flaked almonds
¾ cup glacé cherries, halved
1 cup unsalted roasted peanuts
300g (10oz/1⅓ cups) dark
chocolate, melted

Florentines

Makes approximately 18 florentines

Preheat oven to 150°C (300°F) and line two trays with baking paper.

In a small saucepan, combine milk, honey, butter and sugar and heat until bubbling around the sides.

Add flour and stir out any lumps, cooking for a further 2 minutes then set aside.

In a large mixing bowl, combine all remaining ingredients and pour in the wet mix.

Stir well, then spoon tablespoon size dollops of mixture onto the trays and bake at 150°C (300°F) for 5–7 minutes.

Rotate the trays every 2–3 minutes for even cooking.

Once cooked, remove form the oven and allow to cool completely on the trays.

Spread the bottoms with the melted chocolate and allow to set in the refrigerator for approximately 15–20 minutes.

The Bounty Room

Not So Sweet

Filling

1 tablespoon olive oil
1 brown onion, finely diced
1 tablespoon minced garlic
500g (1lb) lean beef mince
1 medium potato, peeled and diced
2 carrots, peeled and diced
2 teaspoons corn flour
⅔ cup beef stock
2 tablespoons tomato paste
2 tablespoons Worcestershire sauce
2 tablespoons sea salt
2 tablespoons ground lack pepper
2 organic free-range eggs

Pastry

250g (8oz/1¼ cup) diced cold butter
800g (1½ lb) plain flour, sifted
1 teaspoon salt
250-300ml (8-9½fl oz) cold soda water

Cornish Beef Pasties

Makes approximately 35 mini pasties

Make the filling first: in a large frying pan, heat the oil and add onion and garlic, cooking until the onion becomes transluscent, about 3 minutes.

Turn up the heat and add the mince and cook until browned.

Add potatoes and carrots and cook until tender.

In a bowl, combine cornflour and cold stock with a whisk then add to the pan with tomato paste and Worcester sauce. Bring to the boil and turn down to a simmer, until thickened.

Remove from the heat, season and set aside.

Make the pastry: Preheat oven to 180°C (350°F).

In a large bowl, rub together butter, flour and salt until resembling breadcrumbs. Add soda water and work through until a soft dough has formed.

Roll pastry out onto a floured bench and cut into 12cm (5 in) rounds.

Spoon mince mixture onto each round and brush the edges with lightly whisked egg.

Bring pastry edges together to form a semi circle and pinch the edges together forming frills.

Bake for approximately 15–20 minutes.

Tip Short crust pastry can be found in the freezer section of supermarkets as an alternative.

Sausage Rolls

2 teaspoon oil
1 small brown onion finely
chopped
1 garlic clove crushed
500g (1lb) pork mince
2 teaspoon caraway seeds
1 large (2 small) apples (granny
smith are best) grated squeezed to
remove excess moisture
4 teaspoon sea salt
2 teaspoon black pepper
6 sheets frozen puff pastry slightly
thawed
1 egg lightly beaten
nigella seeds to garnish

Chutney

2 small Spanish onions, finely
diced
5 cloves of garlic, finely chopped
12 Roma or egg tomatoes
250ml (8fl oz/1 cup) red wine
vinegar
220g (7¾oz/1 cup) brown sugar

Home Made Sausage Rolls
WITH SPICY TOMATO CHUTNEY

Makes approximately 24 mini sausage rolls

Preheat the oven to 200°C (400°F).

Make the sausage rolls: heat oil in a non-stick saucepan, add onion and garlic and cook stirring until just tender. Set aside and allow to cool.

In a separate bowl combine the mince, caraway seeds, onion mixture, apple, salt and pepper. Mix well.

Place pastry on a workbench and cut in half horizontally so you have two rectangles. Spoon ¼ of the mixture along the long edge of each pastry piece. Brush the pastry edges with the beaten egg and roll tightly to enclose the filling. Cut each roll in half. Brush the tops with egg and sprinkle with nigella seeds.

Place the rolls seam side down on a baking tray lined with greaseproof paper. Repeat with the remaining pastry; mince mixture, egg and nigella seeds.

Bake sausage rolls for 20 minutes or until golden and puffed.

Make the chutney: in a medium saucepan, brown onion and garlic, cooking onion until clear.

Add remaining ingredients and slowly simmer until reduced down to a chutney consistency.

Tip Roll the grated apple in a clean tea towel and twist to squeeze out excess moisture. Nigella seeds can be found in the spice section in all good supermarkets. Use poppy or sesame seeds if you are unable to find Nigella seeds.

750g (1½ lb) salmon fillet
(half roughly chopped, half finely
sliced)
2 organic free-range eggs
zest and juice of 2 limes
2 tablespoons finely chopped dill
1½ tablespoons salt
1 tablespoon white pepper
1 small Spanish onion finely diced
½ cup finely chopped baby capers
35g (1oz) breadcrumbs
10 tablespoons seasoned corn flour
(½ teaspoon salt and ¼ teaspoon
white pepper)
sunflower oil for shallow frying
300g (10oz/1⅓ cups) sour cream
dill springs to serve

Salmon Cakes
WITH SOUR CREAM AND DILL

Makes 16 cakes

Using a food processor, pulse together the roughly chopped salmon with eggs, lime juice and zest and seasoning to form a mousse. Then place in a large bowl.

To the salmon mouse add the finely sliced salmon, dill, onion, capers and breadcrumbs and mix to combine.

Roll quarter cup of the mixture into round patties. Dust with the seasoned cornflour and then shallow fry in oil (medium heat) until cooked and golden—roughly 1–2 minutes each side. Drain on kitchen paper.

Then serve with a dollop of sour cream and springs of dill.

Tip Use fresh Atlantic salmon if you can. Choose fillets that are bright in colour and firm to the touch.

2 teaspoons dry yeast
1 teaspoon castor sugar
250ml (8fl oz) milk, warmed
100g buckwheat flour
100g plain flour, sifted
3 organic free-range eggs,
separated
30g (1oz) melted butter
1 teaspoon white pepper
1 teaspoon sea salt
200g (7oz/1 cup) crème fraîche
400g smoked salmon
50g salmon roe
1 bunch dill, picked
sunflower oil for shallow fying

Smoked Salmon Buckwheat
BLINIS WITH DILL AND CRÈME FRAÎCHE

Makes approximately 24 pikelet size blinis

To make the blinis: combine the yeast and sugar in a small bowl and gradually stir in the warmed milk.

Sift the flour into a large bowl and make a well in the centre.

Add the egg yolks and yeast mixture to the well, then whisk until a smooth batter forms.

Cover with plastic wrap and leave in a warm place for 45 minutes to activate the yeast.

In a saucepan, melt the butter, allow to cool slightly, then stir into the batter. Season with salt and pepper.

In a clean large bowl, beat egg whites until soft peaks form.

Fold through batter until just combined.

Heat a tablespoon of oil in a large, heavy based fry pan over a medium heat.

Drop one teaspoon of batter into the pan, leaving 3cm between each blini.

Cook for 1 minute, or until bubbles form on the surface, then turn and cook for a further 30 seconds.

Remove and repeat with remaining batter, adding oil as required.

Spread 1 teaspoon of crème fraîche on each blini and top with smoked salmon and ¼ teaspoon of the salmon roe and a sprig of dill.

Avocado Salsa

3 ripe avocados, deseeded and
finely diced
4 tomatoes finely diced
1 Spanish (red) onion, finely diced
juice of 2 limes
juice of 2 lemons
50ml (2fl oz/¼ cup) extra virgin
olive oil
1 bunch fresh coriander, chopped
1 small birds eye chilli, finely diced
salt and pepper to taste

125g (4½oz, 1 cup) self-raising
flour, sifted
1 teaspoon sea salt
1 teaspoon white pepper
1 teaspoon sweet paprika
1 teaspoon smoky paprika
4 sweet corn cobs, cooked and
kernels removed and chopped
6 sprigs of shallots, sliced
1 bunch fresh coriander, chopped
2 organic free-range eggs
½ cup coconut cream
200g (7oz) thinly sliced pancetta,
roasted and broken slightly for
garnish

Sweet Corn Cakes
WITH CRISP PANCETTA AND AVOCADO SALSA

Makes approximately 24 pikelet-size corn cakes

Make the salsa by combining all ingredients in a large bowl and mix
together well.

To make the corn cakes: sift flour and mix in salt, pepper and
paprikas.

In a large bowl, beat together eggs and coconut cream and slowly
add flour to form a smooth batter.

Mix in chopped sweet corn, sliced shallots and coriander and set
aside.

In a heavy-based frypan, heat a small amount of oil and drop
spoonfuls of the batter into the pan, cooking over a low heat until
bubbles appear on the surface and are golden underneath. Flip them
over and cook until firm to the touch.

Spoon salsa mix on top of the corn cakes and top with the crisp
pancetta.

2 onions, diced, to make 1 cup
200ml (6½fl oz, 1 cup) olive oil
4 organic free-range eggs
2 cups chopped kalamata olives
1 teaspoon minced garlic
2 tablespoons sugar
250g (8oz/1 cup) grated haloumi cheese
1 teaspoon baking soda
½ teaspoon baking powder
½ teaspoon black pepper
375g (4oz, 3 cups) plain flour
300g (1 cup) sour cream
1 tablespoon fresh, chopped rosemary

Olive, Haloumi
AND ROSEMARY LOAF

Makes approximately 10–12 slices

Preheat oven to 180°C (350°F) and line a 25 x 10 x 10cm (10 x 4 x 4inch) loaf tin.

Sauté onions in oil with garlic and then add chopped olives and rosemary, stir, then set aside to cool.

In a large bowl, beat eggs, and sugar until sugar is dissolved, then add sour cream and mix with cooked onions and olives.

Slowly add sifted flour whisking out any lumps, forming a smooth batter.

Fold through the cheese and seasoning.

Pour into loaf tin and bake for 45–60 minutes or until a skewer comes out cleanly from the centre.

Tip This is great with soft feta and roast tomato and capsicum relish.

250g (8oz/1¼ cup) softened, unsalted butter
250g (8oz/1 cup) grated Parmesan cheese
250g (8oz/1 cup) grated aged cheddar cheese
4 organic free-range eggs
315g (11¼oz/2½ cups) plain flour, sifted
2 teaspoon cayenne pepper
1 bunch fresh thyme

Thyme and Cheddar
BISCUITS

Makes 45 mini biscuits or approximately 24 pikelet-sized cookies

Preheat oven to 180°C (350°F) and line 2 large baking trays with baking paper.

Place butter and cheeses into a bowl and mix with an electric beater until well combined.

Add 2 of the eggs and continue to beat.

Stir in the flour and cayenne pepper.

Place the dough on a floured bench and kneed until smooth.

Place on a sheet of baking paper, with another sheet on the top and roll out the dough to 1cm (½ in) thick and then cut your biscuit.

Place on the baking trays and brush with slightly whisked remaining eggs and sprinkle with thyme.

Bake for 13–15 minutes.

Tip For extra bite, add a little extra cayenne or ground chilli.

Cocktails

High Tea is always pleasant finished with a fine cocktail or two.

1 sprig mint
5 cm (3inches) cucumber, chopped
3 strawberries
½ each of an apple, orange and lemon
Pimm's to taste
Soda water to taste

Pimm's Cup

Makes one jug

In a pitcher or jug, place all fruit ingredients and half fill with ice.

Fill ⅓ of jug with Pimm's.

Fill the remaining portion with soda water or if you have a sweet tooth, lemonade.

For a spicier cup use Ginger Beer instead.

Stir and serve.

1 sprig mint
2 fresh lychees
2 tablespoons rose syrup
Cranberry juice to taste
1 lychee to garnish
fresh mint to garnish

English Rose Mocktail
(Non-Alcoholic)

Makes 1 glass

Rip up mint, add lychees and press with the back of a spoon or any blunt instrument.

Next add rose syrup. You can find this in many delis, particularly those which sell French goods or lots of pastry ingredients.

Finally top with cranberry juice, add some ice, stir and serve with a fresh lychee and some fresh mint on the top.

Hot Gin Punch

Use teacups for this recipe as a measurement:
3 cups gin (a decent gin, try to find one that says 'London Dry Gin' on the bottle or ask your friendly bottle shop attendant)
1 cup sweet red vermouth (any Italian brand will do, Martini and Cinzano are both easy to obtain)
1 pinch of grated nutmeg,
1 pinch of cinnamon powder,
4 slices of lemon (squeeze into mixture),
2 tablespoons of honey,
2 cups of water

Makes 6 tea cups

This potation is said to have been favoured by Charles Dickens himself. You can prepare this on the stove or for a novel manner of serving add all ingredients to a tea pot then add the water already boiled.

If preparing on the stove bring all to a gentle simmer but do not allow it to simmer for more than a few seconds. You just want to heat it and ensure all ingredients are mixed well. If you boil it you will lose the alcohol.

If preparing in a teapot add all ingredients except the water, which is to be boiled separately. Add the boiling water to the mixture in the pot, stir to ensure it is well mixed and serve.

Each tea cup should be served with a wedge of lemon so that your guests can freshen each drink to their taste.

*Light flavoured tea such as
Darjeeling
1 cup boiling water
1 cup gin
2 cups soda water
slices of citrus to serve*

Iced Tea

Makes 4 glasses

What celebratory afternoon tea would not be complete without an iced tea or two? This recipe can be easily added to should you like more flavours, such as peach, mint, or cucumber.

Steep tea in boiling water. After a few minutes strain and chill in the refrigerator. It can be handy to do this in much larger batches and keep on hand in the refrigerator.

Add gin and soda water.

Serve over ice with slices of fresh citrus in each glass.

1 egg
2 tablespoons Scotch whisky
1 tablespoon honey
1 teaspoon absinth (optional)
2 teasoons sweet red Vermouth
1 tablespoon cream (optional)
fresh nutmeg to garnish

Whisky Flip

Makes 4 drinks

In a large mixing bowl, for each serve add egg, whisky and honey.

For those who enjoy a touch more extravagance add absinthe and sweet red vermouth.

If this all sounds too strong, you can quieten the spirit with a tablespoon of cream.

Beat all ingredients with a whisk or electric blender until smooth and you should have a nice thick foam on the surface.

Portion out and grate fresh nutmeg onto the surface of each drink. If no fresh nutmeg is available a pinch of cinnamon will suffice.

This is for those with a higher tolerance to alcohol, or those with a mature palate for whom drinking whisky is of no consequence. This is nice served in a small wine glass.

*700ml bottle of English style rum
from the Caribbean
2 litres of grapefruit juice
juice of four lemons.
10 healthy dashes of Angostura
Bitters
200ml Cherry brandy or sugar
syrup
chopped fruit, such as citrus and
pineapple*

Planter's Punch

For one large punch bowl

Rumpunch became popular throughout the respective empires with no wealthy, self-respecting family without their own punch bowl. We loosely follow the Barbadian rhyming recipe: One of sour, two of sweet, three of strong, four of weak.

Pour rum into punchbowl and add grapefuit juice and lemon juice.

Add Angostura Bitters and cherry brandy.

If you choose to use sugar syrup firstly prepare this by cooking up equal parts water and sugar (eg. 2 cups boiling water, 2 cups sugar) until all the sugar has dissolved. Do not allow to boil or your syrup will be to thick.

Go slow and taste as you add it. When it starts to taste the balance between sweet and sour stop, and always remember who your guests are. If it is for your sister who has just turned 21 chances are she likes a fair bit of sugar, if this is for your father's 60th birthday chances are he likes it quite tart.

Add some chopped fruit of the season to make the punch festive.

Finally add some ice or chill in the refrigerator well in advance and serve out using a ladle.

Index

WEIGHTS AND MEASURES USED IN THIS BOOK

Metric	Imperial
10 g	1/3oz
15 g	½oz
20 g	2/3oz
30 g	1oz
45 g	1½ oz
60 g	2oz
80g	2½oz
90g	3oz
100 g	3½oz
125 g	4oz
150 g	5oz
165 g	5½oz
180 g	6oz
200 g	6½oz
250 g	8oz
300 g	10oz
350 g	11½oz
400 g	13oz
500 g	1 lb
750 g	1½ lb
1 kg	2 lb

Metric	Imperial	Standard Cups
30 ml	1 fl oz	2 tablespoons
60 ml	2 fl oz	¼ cup
80 ml	2¾ fl oz	1/3 cup
125 ml	4 fl oz	½ cup
250 ml	8 fl oz	1 cup
500 ml	16 fl oz	2 cups
750 ml	24 fl oz	3 cups
1 L	32 fl oz	4 cups

Grams per cup	
Butter	230
Buttermilk	250
Flour, all purpose	125
Oil, olive	200
Salt, table	300
Sugar, brown	220
Sugar, powdered (unsifted)	120

First published in Australia in 2010 by New Holland Publishers (Australia) Pty Ltd
Sydney • Auckland • London • Cape Town
1/66 Gibbes Street Chatswood NSW 2067 Australia
218 Lake Road Northcote Auckland New Zealand
86 Edgware Road London W2 2EA United Kingdom
80 McKenzie Street Cape Town 8001 South Africa
Copyright © 2010 New Holland Publishers (Australia) Pty Ltd

A record of this book is held at the National Library of Australia

ISBN 9781741109481

Commissioning Editor: Diane Jardine
Publishing Manager: Lliane Clarke
Designer: Tania Gomes
Proofreading: Meryl Potter
Photographs: Karen Watson
Cover photograph: Karen Watson
Food stylist: Virginia Dowzer
Production Manager: Olga Dementiev
Printed by Toppan Leefung Printing Ltd (China)

10 9 8 7 6 5 4 3 2